SCANDINAVIAN
MYTHOLOGY

H.R.Ellis Davidson

SCANDINAVIAN MYTHOLOGY

PAUL HAMLYN
LONDON · NEW YORK · SYDNEY · TORONTO

Contents

The Hamlyn Publishing Group Limited
London New York Sydney Toronto
Hamlyn House Feltham Middlesex England

Colour plates

Frontispiece: part of a woven tapestry of about A.D. 1100, from Skog Church, Hälsingland, Sweden. The three standing figures in long tunics and hats or helmets have been taken for the trio of gods worshipped by the pagan Swedes, Odin, Thor and Freyr. Odin, with one eye, is on the left, with a tree beside him, although he carries an axe instead of a spear. The central figure has a hammer, and should therefore be Thor. The third holds what might represent fruit or an ear of corn, and could be Freyr, with the small figure of the goddess beside him.

Introduction

We tend to think of Scandinavian mythology as the beliefs of the Vikings, those tough adventurers who were the scourge of Christian lands in the ninth and tenth centuries, whose ships sailed all the seas of the known world, and who left traces of their activities from Greenland to the Volga, and from the Mediterranean to the North American seaboard. The splendid literature which survives from the Middle Ages, written down in monasteries after the conversion to Christianity of the North, gives a vivid picture of their kings and adventurers and the early settlers of Iceland. The stories of their gods and giants and legendary heroes deserve to be more widely known. Their strength and imaginative power, humour, clear-sightedness and sombre magnificence surely merit a place for them beside the myths of ancient Greece and Rome, on which we have long brought up our children.

The religion of the North

The mythology of the North, however, goes back long before the Vikings. Its beginnings may be seen in the Scandinavian Bronze Age, which lasted for over a thousand years, from about 1600 to 450 B.C. In this period enormous advances in art and craftsmanship were made in the Scandinavian lands, as is shown by the fine works in metal and stone which have survived into our own time. It is in the Bronze Age that for the first time we discern recognisable figures of gods and goddesses, and catch glimpses of myth and ritual, although no written sources survive to tell us what language the worshippers spoke. Then after an obscure period about which archaeology can tell us little came a second epoch rich in religious symbolism, the time of transition when all western Europe was in ferment. This period, generally known as the Migration period, lasted from about the third to the sixth centuries A.D. It was the time of the disruption of the Roman Empire, when the Celtic and Germanic peoples were moving westwards and northwards, bringing with them new religious cults and symbols, and fresh viewpoints on the gods. It was then that the cult of Wodan or Odin, the fierce god of death and battle, inspiration and magic lore, flourished in the North. Still we have no written sources, other than brief runic inscriptions, but we have a number of accounts by Greek or Latin writers, and one invaluable book written by the Roman historian Tacitus at the end of the first

Preceding page: the Scandinavian world, with memories of its sacred places and strange mythological creatures, as seen by a map-maker of the sixteenth century. From a copy of the *Carta Marina* of Olaus Magnus, 1539, in the University Library at Uppsala.

Viking head carved in wood on the wagon from the Oseberg ship burial in Norway, which took place in the late ninth century A.D. The wagon has a number of carvings which seem to have religious significance, and it was presumably used at the funeral. Ship Museum, Byggdøe, near Oslo.

century A.D. He was sufficiently impressed by what he learned concerning the Germanic peoples on the borders of the Empire to write an account of their way of life. The evidence of archaeology and heroic poetry indicate that this way of life continued during the Migration period much as he described it.

The Germans lived in small warrior tribes under aristocratic leaders, sometimes following them to new kingdoms in search of adventure and plunder and lands on which to settle.

monsters dwelt, and of the constant threat to their precarious little world once the forces of chaos were unleashed. Their experience of a savage world in which kingdoms were constantly set up and destroyed, with a background of stormy seas and long, cold winter nights, gave a sombre tinge to their picture of the realm of the gods, but at the same time it imparted a sturdy vigour to the figures who people their myths.

At the end of the Migration period small

Impressionistic human figure carved on a rock at Ausevik, Sogn, Norway. He forms part of a large group of animals and abstract symbols, but remains on the edge of this. It seems likely that he represents either a shaman or a guardian spirit.

They were proud of their oral traditions about the kings and heroes of the past; they held high ideals of courage in battle and loyalty to their leaders and to their kindred; they respected and honoured their womenfolk; and they valued traditional laws which were believed to have been established by the gods they worshipped. Their outstanding deities ruled the battlefield and extorted heavy sacrifices from their worshippers, gave them good seasons, rich crops and prosperity, and had power over the realm of the sky, the thunder and the life-bringing rain. They were very conscious also of the grim underworld where the giants and

settled kingdoms were established in Scandinavia and Britain, one of the most impressive being that of the Uppland kings of Sweden, whose burial place was a centre of sanctity in the seventh century. The Anglo-Saxons were converted early to Christianity, as were the continental Germans. But in Scandinavia paganism lived on for several centuries, and received a new impetus in the vigorous period of adventure and conquest known as the Viking Age. As the Scandinavians ventured further afield in the ninth and tenth centuries in search of trade, adventure, piracy or new homelands for the younger sons and the dispossessed, they carried the cults of their heathen gods with them, but at the same time they came under new influences from the lands to which their journeyings led them. They learned something from the practices of their Christian neighbours, wearing the hammer of Thor as the Christians wore the cross, raising impressive stone memorials like those which they saw in their travels and possibly building temples of carved wood in emulation of the stone churches. The bloodthirsty cults of the eastern lands which they reached by way of the Russian rivers seem to have given them a new enthusiasm for human and animal sacrifice, especially in honour of the god Odin, god of death and magic, who was still worshipped at Uppsala along with Freyr, the god of fertility, and Thor, the ruler of the thunder. The Viking poets and storytellers knew many good tales, both serious and comic, about these gods, the powerful but fickle goddesses, and the giants who continually sought to overthrow the kingdom of Asgard.

The sources

It is, however, important to remember that these stories have for the most part reached us in the work of Christian writers, and that much of the original heathen tradition was edited, misunderstood or forgotten before the myths reached us. The only written statements left by pagan men are short runic inscriptions on wood, bone, stone or metal. These, while they provide important evidence, tend to be cryptic both in syntax and thought, and therefore extremely difficult to interpret, particularly when they take the form of spells or curses or allusions to mythical beings. This is true also of the earliest skaldic poems, short alliterative verses packed with mythological allusions, which were composed by poets who lived before the conversion. We get an occasional glimpse of the life of the Vikings and their religious customs through the eyes of Latin writers, or Arab travellers who visited their settlements and trading centres. But such reporting is apt to be brief and unsympathetic, and to leave out the very things we most want to know. Therefore we must depend largely, even for this late period, on archaeological evidence about the symbols and characteristics of the gods, the places where men gathered to worship them, religious rites and burial customs. This evidence helps greatly towards the fuller understanding of the tangled evidence of the myths recorded in a Christian

age. Further knowledge can be gained from the study of place-names and of the names and epithets of the gods in early poetry. In addition, the history of religions and myths outside Scandinavia enables us to see the evidence in a truer perspective.

Saxo and Snorri

In the early days of Scandinavian Christianity, two scholars, a Dane and an Icelander, set to work to collect and record some of the old

King Gylfi of Sweden confronts three mysterious powers who can give him information about the ancient gods. From an early manuscript of the *Prose Edda* of Snorri Sturluson in the University Library at Uppsala. Snorri's book is one of the main sources for the northern myths.

stories still current about the gods and goddesses. The first was an ecclesiastic historian of the twelfth century, Saxo Grammaticus, who included many tales about the gods in the first six books of a lengthy history of Denmark, told in a heavy Latin style which is difficult to read. He appears to have had little love for the legends, and to have found many of the doings of the gods and early heroes stupid and distasteful, but he has preserved many stories and traditions which we would otherwise have lost.

Very different was the second writer, Snorri Sturluson, a brilliant poet and historian as well as an active politician, who wrote in his native Icelandic. About the year 1220, he produced a handbook for poets, so that they would recognise allusions to the myths and use them correctly. Possibly he felt some indignation at his predecessor's clumsy treatment of the gods, for he recorded the old myths with love and enthusiasm. He wrote in controlled, ironic prose far ahead of most of his European contemporaries, with a full appreciation of the imaginative beauty and the dry humour of the tales he told. His *Prose Edda* was so successful that our knowledge of the northern myths is largely derived from it, and where we have been able to check his information from surviving poetry, it is surprisingly accurate. But Snorri was writing over two hundred years after Christianity was accepted by the Icelandic Assembly in the year 1000, and the myths presented him with many unsolved problems, as they do us, so that owing to the limitations of his knowledge he may at times unintentionally mislead us.

The poems

All too few mythological poems have survived, most of them contained in one precious manuscript, the Codex Regius, found in an Icelandic farmhouse in the seventeenth century, and generally known as the *Elder* or *Poetic Edda*. In the poems about the gods which form half of this collection, the supernatural beings encounter giants and dwarfs, take part in dialogues and riddle contests, and outwit one another in comic or tragic conflicts. The poems culminate in the destruction of the worlds of gods and men in the great disaster of Ragnarok.

Prose works

Something further may be learned from other prose sources. The sagas or prose histories of

the early kings of Norway and Sweden, retold by Snorri Sturluson and others from earlier traditions and poems, give a vivid picture of the conversion of Norway and tell us something of what went before. The Icelandic sagas are stories of the early settlers of Iceland, who were heathens of the ninth and tenth centuries. These sagas too are based partly on early oral traditions, but partly also on the ideas of gifted storytellers of the thirteenth century about what heathen Iceland was like. The legendary sagas, 'stories of old time', are even more mixed in their content, and contain romance material from abroad mingled with early native traditions recorded in a confused form, with fleeting echoes of heroic stories and tales of ancient kings and heroes in Scandinavia and the north of Russia.

Archaeology and art

Thus while our knowledge of Scandinavian mythology is continually increasing, it must be clearly understood at the outset that our understanding of it is limited by the confused and incomplete nature of our sources. We owe much to the work of archaeologists in recent years, and the evidence which they have provided will be drawn on constantly throughout this book. There were three centres of ancient tradition, Sweden, Norway and Denmark, where the mythology can be tentatively traced back to its early beginnings. In the ninth century A.D. Iceland was colonised, mainly from Norway. It proved a wonderfully fertile source for stories and poems, and many of our written records

Left: gold bracteate of the sixth century from Gerete, Gotland. It elaborates the theme of the Emperor on horseback, as on Roman medallions. The rows of watching faces, as well as the symbols surrounding the central figure, are typically northern in treatment. Such bracteates were amulets intended to bring luck and protection, and they show various symbols associated with the northern gods.

Some idea of the timber halls of the Viking Age can be gained from this reconstruction of one of the buildings at Trelleborg, a military camp of about the year 1000 on Zealand in Denmark.

Above: a fiord at Gloppedalsur in Norway dominated by mountains and rocks.

Above right: a Swedish landscape at Kalmar in eastern Sweden, where an inlet of the Baltic stretches far into the land.

Right: a typical Scandinavian home: reconstruction of a hut in an Iron Age village at the Archaeological Research Centre at Lejre, Denmark.

come from the early monasteries there. Yet Iceland was settled fairly late in the heathen period, and the essential links with the holy places of the Scandinavian homelands were cut, so that archaeologically our debt to Iceland is much less than to Sweden, where the old gods ruled up to the beginning of the twelfth century. Some evidence comes from outside Scandinavia, from the early settlements of the Vikings and particularly those in the British Isles, from which come some of the finest carved stones inspired by the pagan myths. On the other side of Europe, Swedish settlers along the Volga and the Dnieper on the way to Byzantium and the East were still heathen, and we hope to learn more of them from excavations round Kiev and Novgorod. In particular, the Baltic island of Gotland, which lies on the direct route between Sweden and the eastern settlements, has proved to be a treasure-house of religious symbolism, because of its rich collection of heathen memorial stones dating from the fifth century to the end of the Viking Age.

Outside Scandinavia

Links with other Germanic peoples are also of great importance, and the discovery of the great treasure of Sutton Hoo has revealed how close were the bonds between Swedish Uppland and the Anglo-Saxon kingdom of East Anglia in the seventh century, the last century when it was possible for Anglo-Saxons to practice the cults of the heathen gods without being harried by Christian priests. The symbolism of the Sutton Hoo royal grave shows a mixture of heathen and Christian tradition which will provide us with problems for a long time to come. Certainly archaeological evidence from England has helped to throw light on the paganism of the North, just as the great heroic epic of the Anglo-Saxons, *Beowulf*, which has a Scandinavian background for its heroes and monsters, has revealed something of the early history of the kings of Denmark and Sweden. More evidence comes from Germany, where heathenism lingered in pockets after the Christian church was established there, leaving occasional traces in the form of carved stones and heathen cemeteries as well as the spells and stories of supernatural beings which survived into Christian times.

Thus the story of Scandinavian mythology has to be built up cautiously and patiently from many different sources and by many varying methods. Gradually a picture emerges, and we find it, as did Snorri Sturluson in the thirteenth century, a moving and exciting one. The gods of the North, whose roots, like those of their own World Tree, go down into the darkness of the past, are deities to command our respect and stir our imagination. The courage and loyalty and determination of the Vikings have long won admiration, in spite of the reckless destruction and cruelty which was the other side of the coin. Moreover, the faith which they practised was no superficial one. It lasted well over a thousand years in the North, and has in it not a little wisdom. It was born out of the thoughts and aspirations of men born into a tough world and reared in a hard climate. They had learned to adapt themselves to life, and for the most part undoubtedly found it good, steeling themselves to face its blows when they came without flinching, and to waste no time in vain regrets. Thus for all our advances in knowledge and sophistication, we may indeed have something to learn from Scandinavian mythology.

The coming of the gods

The first men who inhabited Scandinavia lived as hunters, fishers and food-gatherers, and they have left traces of their religious practices in the form of great animal carvings on the rocks. These are found in remote, sometimes almost inaccessible places, along the cliffs of the rocky Norwegian coast, beside rivers and waterfalls and glaciers, or on rocks out in the water. The most impressive of these carvings are enormous naturalistic figures of bears, elk and reindeer. There are also strange diagrammatic figures of animals, mixed with abstract symbols, shapes of birds and fishes, and occasional man-made objects such as boats, sledges and weapons. The semi-human figures which sometimes appear may well represent powers of the spirit world. But when we find a figure seemingly bound and asleep, like one carved on a reindeer horn from the Maglemose period, about 6000 B.C., or in a wild dance, like several figures from Norway, it seems reasonable to suggest that they are men taking part in magical shamanistic rites, especially since they sometimes wear horned head-dresses as a link with the animal world. It is to be presumed that the early hunters, like men following a similar way of life in other parts of the world, were led in their religion by shamans rather than priests. These were men of their tribe who shared their life, but who were closely linked with the animal and the spirit worlds. They could dance themselves into a state of ecstasy and formed a link between men and the powers that ruled life and death for both animals and humans.

Megalithic tombs

Not until men learnt to live in villages and to practise a simple form of agriculture, with domesticated animals and cereal crops for a staple food, do we find traces of organised cults. They were linked with the agricultural year and holy places where ceremonial rites could be performed. Such holy places were the great tombs of the dead in the late Neolithic period in Scandinavia. In these collective graves were stored the bones of ancestors.

It would seem that the chief deity whom the villagers worshipped was the goddess of the earth, the Earth Mother, who received her children back into the welcoming tomb. It was she who made the earth fertile, and brought increase to flocks and herds, and healthy children to the tribe. At first there is little indication as to how these early people pictured their goddess,

Two helmets of the late Bronze Age found in a peat bog at Viksø, Zealand. The curved horns resemble those of the little bronze man from Grevens Vaeng, believed to represent the sky god, while the staring eyes and beak suggest a bird of prey. National Museum, Copenhagen.

with ornaments of fine metalwork. From this period we find clear evidence of ritual from many symbolic objects recovered from the earth, and from the rich and crowded pictures of what appear to be religious ceremonies on the rock surfaces of Scandinavia. Now for the first time we find clear traces of a deity or deities connected with the sky and with battle, the god of a warrior people whose year was governed by the movements of the sun. The axe, already venerated in the Neolithic period as man's most treasured tool and weapon, is brandished in the hands of a powerful phallic figure, dominating lesser figures on the rocks. A giant figure is also shown with a spear in his hand, and spears and axes are represented many times as if they were sacred symbols, linked with the divine powers. In the nineteenth century two small

Above: a reindeer carved on rock in realistic style at Bøla in Trondelag, northern Norway. It is about two yards long, and is one of the impressive animal carvings made by the hunting peoples in many remote parts of Norway and Sweden.

Right: carving of a fish on a rock at Buskerud, Norway. The style of carving is different from that of the huge animal silhouettes. The outline has been divided up by a complex series of lines which may suggest scales.

although sometimes we get a glimpse of a sombre face with staring eyes on pots placed in the graves. The narrow passages of stone leading into the awe-inspiring megalithic burial chambers of the largest graves suggest the symbol of the womb of the Earth Mother, into which the dead returned. Pots and urns, deliberately smashed to fragments, have been left in the graves, in particular round the curved, horn-shaped entrances, implying elaborate rites held at the gate of the tomb itself. It seems probable that the cleansed bones of the dead, after being kept outside for a while until the flesh decayed, were carried down the low, narrow passage into the tomb at the time of the dead person's final purification and departure from the community to the spirit world of the ancestors. Certainly the opening of the tombs must have been an awesome ceremonial. The doors, whether in the form of a capstone or set at the end of the passage, are thought to have been left uncovered by the earth, so that the way of entry was always open. Regular rites may also have been held in or near the tombs at regular times throughout the agricultural year or at certain periods of the lunar cycle.

Bronze Age religion

In the Bronze Age, however, the people who became the ruling class in Denmark and Sweden and southern Norway did not bury their dead in megalithic tombs, but placed them in burial mounds standing up against the sky-line. The graves commemorated heroes laid with their weapons beside them, and high-born women

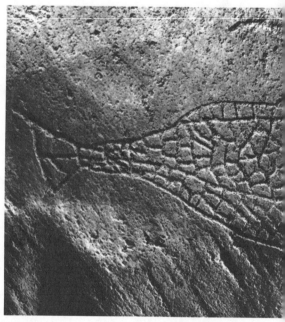

bronze figures of men with axes in their hands and wearing helmets set with horns, a sign of power, were found in Denmark, although only one, without his axe, now survives. These date from the late Bronze Age.

The sky god and the sun disc

The axe must be associated with the god who ruled the sky and sent thunder and lightning and the life-giving rain. Whether the spear-bearing figure represented him in another aspect, as leader in battle and giver of victory, we do not know for certain, but this seems probable. These male figures and the weapons which

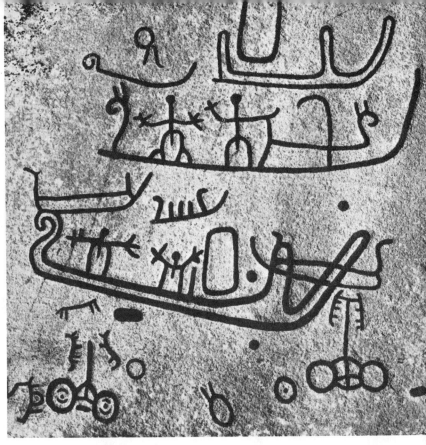

they carry are connected constantly in the carvings with ships and horses. It seems that the primary myth of the northern Bronze Age concerned the wheeled wagon or chariot of the sun journeying across the heavens, and also the ship of the sun, which is thought to have symbolised the sun's journey beneath the earth when it disappeared beneath the western sea. This belief is confirmed by the discovery of a small model of a wagon bearing a disc, beautifully ornamented and gilded on one side, at Trundholm in Denmark. A horse was found with it, probably one of a pair, and there are references to other finds of similar vehicles, now lost. Wagons are frequently pictured on the rocks, drawn by horned beasts, or alone, and seem to be in themselves sacred symbols. The disc, often resembling a wheel, is shown contin-

spokes, like a wheel. It is hardly surprising to find that the birds of the Bronze Age associated with the sun disc were water-birds, the wild ducks and swans which could fly far and fast through the sky and also swim and dive under the waves. The mysterious beauty and sense of power conveyed by these wild birds in flight must have been very familiar to Bronze Age man among the many marshes and rivers of Denmark and Sweden.

The sacred ship

Sometimes the ship contained a human figure, and sometimes a lively crew, holding weapons or musical instruments, or taking part in wild dances or acrobatics. The implication would seem to be that such model ships, as well as wagons, appeared in cult processions. Sometimes a ship is held in the hand of a god or a worshipper, and ships were evidently associated with the world of the dead. There are ships, horses and axes depicted on the slabs of the impressive grave chamber at Bredoror in Kivik, in south-west Sweden. The great tumulus must have been made for some powerful priest-king, but unhappily it was rifled of its contents and extensively damaged by treasure-hunters in the eighteenth century. Some of the Bronze Age dead, both men and women, were laid to rest in tree-coffins, made from the hollowed trunks of large oaks, which closely resemble the tree-canoes of the Bronze Age. They may also have typified the ship of the sun, in which certain privileged dead were carried to the Other World.

A Bronze Age rock carving from Borge in Østfold, Norway, of ships, some carrying a pair of human figures with outstretched hands, and of wagons, drawn diagramatically. The circle beside each wagon may represent the sun disc which it carried.

ually, sometimes held up as if for adoration, and sometimes borne by tiny men like a shield, or given hands and feet. It is sometimes placed on or above a ship, and ships are also associated with both horses and birds. Models of chariots drawn by birds have been found in central and eastern Europe, and these may represent a different interpretation of the journey of the sun, which has influenced Scandinavian art, but been replaced in the North by the symbol of the wagon. It was in the Bronze Age that the wheel was first introduced into Scandinavia, and it must have been in itself a symbol of power: indeed the disc of the sun is often shown with

Below: drawings of
four bronze figures
from Grevens Vaeng in
Zealand made by Brandt
in 1778 soon after their
discovery. The figures
appear to represent deities
of the late Bronze Age
and their worshippers.
Only two of them have
survived. Right: girl
bending in a backward
somersault. Far right:
man in horned helmet.
Also shown is a woman
with a bowl from Itzehoe,
Holsten.

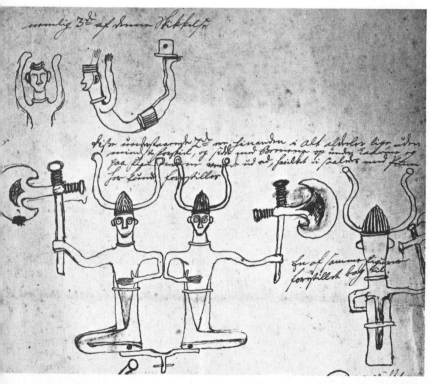

Sacred animals

Among the crowded scenes depicted on the rocks, there are a number of sacred animals. In particular, the great male animals are shown, symbols of the sky god who was the begetter and fecundator, and from these the bull in particular stands out clearly. Some scenes suggest bull sacrifice, and on others men seem to be leaping over the backs of the bulls, as in the illustrations of the Minoan bull games. The boar, the stag and the horse are also prominent in the carvings, and some horses have horns, as if in imitation of bulls or stags. The horns of the powerful wild creatures, such as the great reindeer and elk shown in the carvings of the early huntsmen in Norway, were undoubtedly accepted as symbols of force and power, and were imitated in the splendid ceremonial helmets of the Bronze Age found at Viksø in Denmark. Sledges and ploughs and much of the background of farming are also shown on the rocks.

Twin gods

It seems that the god of the sky, associated both with thunder and the sun, was pictured with a twin brother. Such at least seems to be the significance of the twin axe-men and the twin figures which appear in ships. Pairs of both horses and birds also appear as a consistent symbol in the late Bronze Age. Whether this dualism was based on the rising and setting sun or on its twofold journey above and below the earth is hard to say. Parallels to this idea of divine brothers are found in other mythologies, including ancient Egypt, where the ship of the sun was a symbol of great importance. Always, however, they form part of a complex mythological pattern, and we need to know much more of the religion of the northern Bronze Age to understand their full significance.

The goddess

The scenes on the rocks show rites of a predominantly masculine cult, suitable for warriors and farmers, in which women played little part, except presumably to applaud the processions. It is possible however that the ship itself was a symbol of the earth goddess, for she does not disappear as the cult of the sky god develops. On the contrary, we have a number of little figurines of the late Bronze Age, which depict her clearly for the first time. She wears a short skirt, has bare breasts and a neck-ring, and wears her hair in a plait. The most impressive of these little bronze figures, with large eyes of gold, is in a kneeling position, with one arm raised and the fingers of the other hand holding the nipple of her left breast. It has been thought from her posture that she was driving in some wagon or chariot, and a serpent-like creature found with her may have been the animal that she drove. Other female figures carry bowls, kneel with hands on breast, or bend backwards in a somersault like a little figure, one of three, which survives from Grevens Vaeng in Denmark and was found with the axe-men. The goddess is also shown on cremation urns, and in one case she seems to be greeting a male figure with outstretched hands, while her necklace encircles both of them. There is evidence too that offerings in the form of plaits of hair and neck-rings were made in the peat bogs of Denmark in this period. These surely must have been sacrifices to the goddess, though whether they were women's votive offerings or records of human sacrifice we do not know. The implication is that worship of the goddess went on alongside the public ceremonial depicted on the rocks. But this worship may perhaps have been conducted in secret, for initiates only, and concealed from the light of day.

Carving of a bear in silhouette on a rock at Finnhägen in Nordland, Norway.

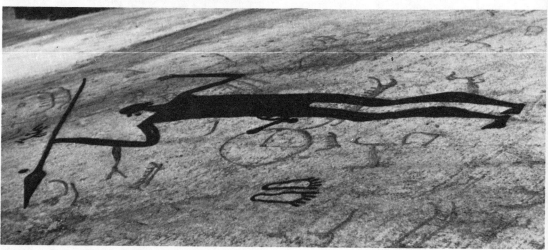

Huge phallic figure brandishing a spear, dominating the other Bronze Age carvings on the rocks at Bohuslän, Sweden. This has been taken for a representation of the supreme sky god who also ruled over the battle field, the Tîwaz of the Germanic peoples. The pair of human feet beside him may also be a symbol of the divine presence. Carvings of ships and smaller figures may be seen in the background.

One of the battered slabs which formed the grave chamber in the great burial mound at Kivik, thought to show scenes of ritual significance connected with the funeral ceremonies. Figures wearing bird masks and blowing horns can be seen, and a group of women or priests approaching a cauldron. One explanation of the two figures at the top left hand corner is that they are using a fire drill.

The divine marriage

The male and female figures on the urn could represent the goddess greeting her worshipper. Or the phallic figure beside her might be the god of the sky, and the scene might symbolise the divine marriage. Other scenes which suggest such a symbolism have been noted on the rocks. In one a large figure raises an axe over a male and female pair standing before him, and in others there is a possible bridal pair with what seems to be a man lying slain beside them. In other scenes a female figure appears to lead others in lamentation, with hands raised aloft. It has been thought that these scenes might depict ceremonies of mourning for a dead god, a rite associated with the departure of the sun, or the death of nature in the autumn of the year. We do not yet know enough about the religion of the northern Bronze Age to be confident about this, nor do we know whether one of the carvings from the Kivik grave represents two men kindling the New Fire, symbolising the return of the sun after the winter darkness. This rite lived on as a folk custom for a long time in central and eastern Europe, and eventually became an integral part of the Easter ritual and ceremonials of the Christian church.

Indeed we know all too little about the beliefs of the men of the Bronze Age, but what is indicated by the archaeological evidence is a well established cult of the god of the sky, together with continued worship of the earth goddess, emphasis on the symbol of the journey of the sun, and ceremonial based on the pattern of the changing year. Further archaeological finds will no doubt add to our knowledge.

Left: a stone in the museum at Lindisfarne Priory on Holy Island in Northumberland. It shows a line of Viking warriors armed with axes. The monastery at Lindisfarne was attacked and burned by Vikings in A.D. 875.

Below: a typical rock carving of the Bronze Age with men, ships, and a sun disc, together with a small animal which is probably a horse.

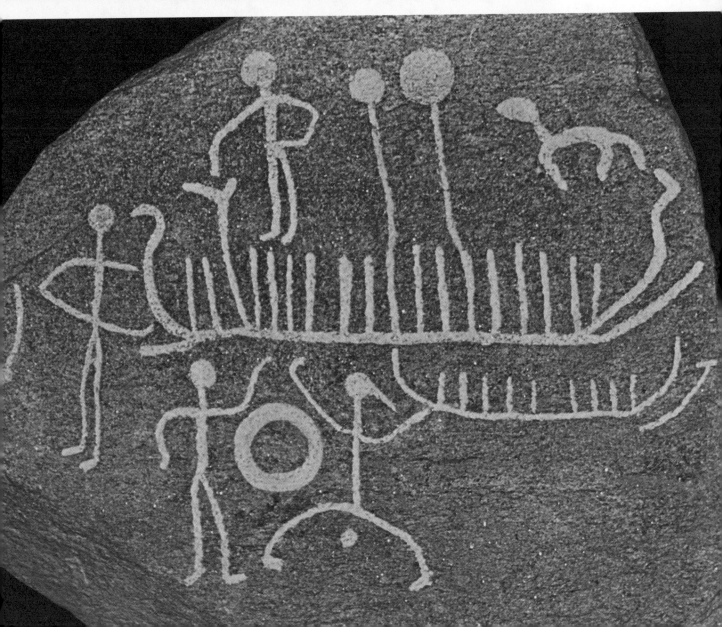

The cult of Odin

In the first centuries after Christ, when the general movement of Celts and Germans was getting under way, there were signs in Denmark of new customs connected with battle and the dead. In rich Danish cemeteries we find the symbolism of a banquet within the grave. The wealthy dead were provided with dishes of meat and goblets or horns of mead and ale, together with an impressive dinner service of cups, plates, jars and knives. Sometimes a wine strainer was given to the dead to hold, or a cup left within reach of the hand. The inspiration for such a custom seems to have come from the aristocratic warriors of the Celts, whose ancestors were buried in the Hallstatt 'wagon graves' further east. Among the Celtic people, the banquet long remained an important ritual, and joints of pork, in particular, were shared out according to strict rules of precedence.

Feasting in Valhalla

It is possible that such customs and the ideas behind them helped to establish the long literary tradition in Scandinavia of the feasting of warriors in Valhalla. Here reigned Odin, god of death and battle (the Wodan of the Germans and Woden of the Anglo-Saxons), who has given his name to the fourth day of the week in Scandinavia and English-speaking countries. He was believed to welcome into his hall warriors who died a heroic death on the battlefield. Each night they feasted on joints of pork from a boar whose flesh never gave out, and drank copiously of mead. The day was spent in fighting, but every night those who had fallen were raised up again to partake of the feast. In the literature the reason given for Odin's hospitality was that he was collecting a mighty host from among the noble dead to follow him in the last great battle, when the gods would have to fight for survival against monsters and giants. His special champions, the *einherjar*, were to lead the ranks of his warriors on that day.

The cult of kings

It was said of Odin that he set kings a-warring, or, as Saxo put it, 'he weaves the dooms of the mighty and fills Phlegthon with noble shapes'. For the worshippers of Odin were the kings and princely warriors of the Migration period and the Viking Age, and many royal families among the Anglo-Saxons were proud to count themselves his descendants. To leaders who promised to dedicate those whom they slew to the god,

Carved head in the stave church at Hegge, Norway. This could be a representation of the one-eyed god Odin. The outstretched tongue would be in keeping with Odin as the god of hanged men.

Overleaf: model of a bronze disc on wheels with a horse (probably one of a pair) to draw it. About sixty centimetres long, found in fragments at Trundholm in Zealand. The disc is gold-plated on one side and is believed to represent the sun travelling across the sky. National Museum, Copenhagen.

he gave out weapons, such as the splendid sword Gram had given to Sigmund the Volsung. Odin himself plunged the sword deep into the tree forming the central pillar of the family hall, so that only the hand of the young hero who had won his favour was able to withdraw it. For many years Sigmund fought heroically for Odin, but at last the end came, when the god decided that it was time for the king to join his warriors in the Other World. Odin himself, as a one-eyed man in a blue cloak and broad-brimmed hat, met him in the midst of the fighting, and shattered the wonderful sword with his own spear.

Saxo has other similar incidents in his collection of stories about the kings of Denmark. On one occasion the same old man with one eye appeared to King Harald War-tooth, and made a pact with him, promising him to grant him victory if Harald would dedicate to him all those whom he slew in battle. But again the day came when Odin withdrew his favour. He stirred up a quarrel with Harald's friend and ally, King Hring, and when the two kings met in battle, he took the place of Harald's charioteer and flung him down from the chariot even as Harald pleaded with him for one further victory. The king was pierced by his own sword as he fell. It is hardly surprising that both in the early poems and in the later prose stories Odin is continually accused of treachery and broken faith, since his promise of victory to his followers was something which, in the very nature of things, could not be kept for ever. In a poem of the tenth century on the death of one of the heathen kings of Norway, Eric Bloodaxe, the god is asked by the hero Sigmund, now in Valhalla, why he had chosen to let Eric be robbed of victory when he was so valiant. Odin's reply is: 'The grey wolf is watching the abode of the gods', and the implication of the myth is clear: the bound monster who was ultimately to devour Odin was waiting for the end to come, since the god himself was not immune from the law of ultimate defeat inherent in our mortality, the law to which even the strongest must eventually bow.

Battle sacrifices

There are many stories of kings making pacts with Odin to deliver to him those killed in battle, and sacrifices to him as god of the dead are frequently mentioned in the literature. Tacitus tells us of two Germanic tribes who fought for

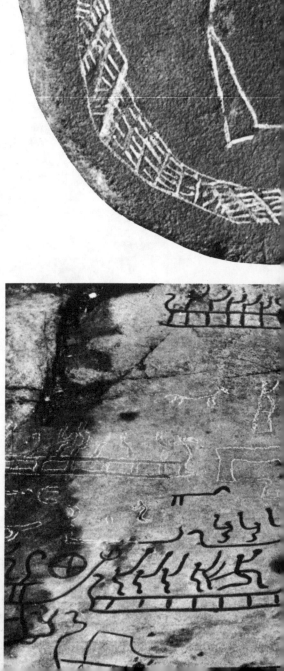

the possession of a sacred place, each vowing to their god that in return for victory they would sacrifice all that they won, men and booty alike; and one of the gods mentioned is Mercury, who is the Roman equivalent for the Germanic god Wodan.

Startling confirmation for such stories comes from the peat bogs of Denmark and Sweden, where, for a period extending from the Celtic Iron Age, shortly before the birth of Christ, to about the sixth century A.D., great offering places were established in the marshes, some of which have now been carefully excavated. The peat has preserved many of the objects laid down in bogs or thrown into pools, and while some of the offerings were associated with agriculture and fertility, there seems no doubt that part of them consisted of plunder from defeated armies. Swords and shields have been found in abundance, as also have coats of mail, spears and bows and arrows, war-canoes like the Hjortspring boat filled with warriors' equipment, along with clothes, ornaments, metal vessels and other valuable possessions which may or may not have been booty taken in war. The weapons and mail were often bent and broken in pieces or burnt on a fire before being left in the place of offering or thrown into the water. Some warriors in Scandinavia evidently acted in the same way as the Celts are described by Caesar to have done in the first century B.C., leaving piles of booty on holy ground, where no man dared tamper with it because a horrible death was the penalty for such sacrilege.

Ritual hanging

Not only inanimate objects have been found in the bogs. Skeletons of horses have been found too, and over the years a gruesome series of human bodies. Some of these, such as the man from Tollund in Denmark whose serene face implies a calm resignation in the face of death, had a rope round the neck, a sign of death by strangulation. Stories from the literature and evidence from foreign writers are in agreement that sacrifices to Odin took place by strangling, while at the same time the victim was stabbed with a spear. The bodies of the men and animals sacrificed were left hanging from trees. Captives in war were said to have been dispatched in this way, and as late as the eleventh century there is an account in the history of Adam of Bremen of bodies of men and animals seen dangling from trees in the sacred grove at Uppsala. The old

Overleaf left: a spearhead of the Viking Age, with delicate inlaid ornament which suggests that it possessed some ceremonial function. The spear was the weapon of the god Odin and a symbol of his cult.

Overleaf right: carving from Vitlycke, Bohuslän, in Sweden, where the familiar sun discs are given arms and legs and transformed into warriors waving axes. It seems probable that these represent followers of the sky-god, either on earth or in the Other World.

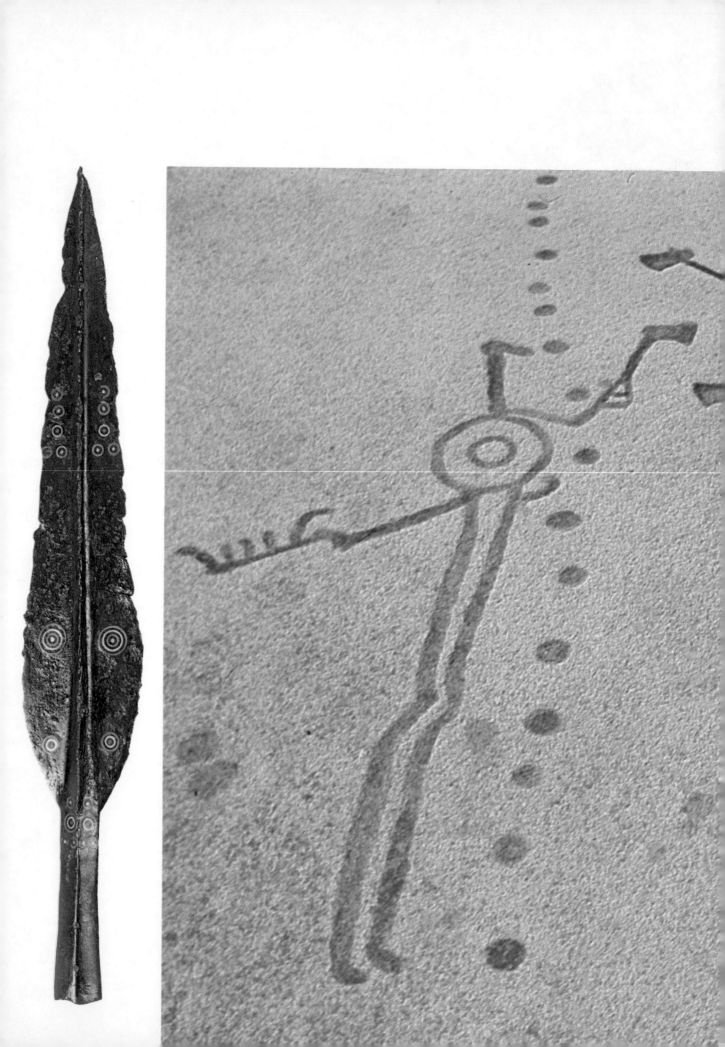

The stag was one of the earliest animals represented in the Scandinavian rock carvings, and was still a powerful symbol in the seventh century A.D. for the royal house of East Anglia. This figure of a young male stag was set on the top of the metal standard from the royal ship-burial at Sutton Hoo in Suffolk. British Museum.

man who provided the information recalled seeing these when he visited the temple.

The most detailed description of this kind of sacrifice comes from the story of the death of a Viking leader, King Vikar, who had prayed to Odin for a favourable wind. He drew lots to decide which of his men was to be sacrificed in return for the granting of his petition. The lot fell upon the king himself, and his men staged a mock sacrifice. They set their leader on a tree stump with a calf's intestines round his neck instead of a rope, looped round a young tree which they held down beside him. The man standing beside the king, who was a faithful follower of Odin, touched Vikar with a rod and uttered the words: 'Now I give you to Odin'. At that instant the soft intestines became a tough rope, and the rod turned into a spear and pierced the king through. The tree shot upwards, with the dead king hanging from it. Such a ritual killing is shown on one of the Gotland stones from the Viking Age. An eagle, the bird of Odin, perches above the victim. It would seem indeed that sacrificial victims were not always captives taken in war. There are grim tales of kings sacrificing their sons to gain their desires. Aun, king of Sweden, was said to offer up one of his sons every ten years to obtain a longer span of life. At length, when he had grown so old that he was as helpless as a child, the Swedes forbade the sacrifice of his last son, and Aun died, without honour. Another vivid little story is that of the woman who asked Odin for help in brewing ale. He asked in return that she should give to him whatever lay between her and the vat. This turned out to be the unborn child she was carrying, whose story is told in the course of the saga.

The spear of Odin

The type of sacrifice most typical of the cult of Odin was that of men killed in battle or put to death by the victors, and the symbol for a warrior's death was the spear. Odin's great treasure was his mighty spear Gungnir, which could determine victory by the direction which it took over the battlefield. On one early stone from Gotland a spear can be seen passing above a ship, so that this conception may go back as early as the Migration period. Long after Christianity came to Iceland it was still thought a lucky omen to throw a spear over the heads of an advancing band of enemies, as described in one of the Icelandic sagas. The spears so frequently buried with men in heathen times, and tiny model spears found in graves of boys or worn as amulets by the dead, may well have been linked with the cult of the god of battle and have been the mark of his followers.

The ring of Odin

Dedicated warriors who fought without defensive armour because they counted themselves under the protection of the god were known among the Germans at the time of Tacitus. He tells us that some of these wore metal collars to show that they were in the god's service. This may explain the magnificent collars formed of bands of gold surviving from the Migration period in Sweden. They are among the greatest treasures of the time. We may see here a link also with another of the treasures of Odin, the self-perpetuating gold ring Draupnir, from which nine new gold rings dropped every ninth night. As a leader in battle, Odin was naturally viewed as a ring-giver, dealing out treasure in the form of gold rings to his followers. Earthly rulers were praised for doing this in the heroic poems. The purse filled with gold coins which formed part of a king's treasures in the ship-burial at Sutton Hoo may be seen as another instance of the same symbolism. There may also be a link with the symbol of three triangles or rings intertwined, known as the *valknut*, which can be seen on the Gotland stones of the Viking Age and elsewhere in association with Odin.

Both *valknut* and rings may indeed symbolise the power of Odin to bind and to loose, which

Symbolic carvings of animals and abstract shapes on rocks at Ausevik, in west Norway.

was especially shown in battle. He was able to
lay fetters of panic, paralysing terror or fatal
hesitation on doomed men, while giving those
he favoured immunity from such bonds by the
wild intoxication which freed warriors from
inhibition and fear. The hero of one of the
Icelandic sagas, the outlaw Hord, was finally
captured because, brave man though he was, a
'war-fetter' came upon him in a fight with his
enemies, and he was unable for a while to defend
himself. He twice fought off this paralysis of the
will, but the third time it overcame him, and
he eventually went down before his enemies'
weapons.

Odin's champions

Pictures of young warriors naked except for a
belt and a horned helmet have survived on Swedish helmet plates of the sixth century, as well
as on a gilded buckle from a seventh-century
Anglo-Saxon grave in Kent. Similar figures were
depicted earlier on one of the famous gold horns
from Gallehus in Denmark. Such warriors carry
a sword and a spear, or a spear in either hand.
They may be taking part in the weapon dance
which Tacitus describes as performed by German
youths between upraised weapons.

The most interesting example of such a figure
is on a helmet-plate from the Valsgärde cemetery
in Sweden, for he is shown leaping on to a
warrior's horse and apparently guiding the rider's spear. In this case it would seem that the
warrior is doomed, since his horse is being stabbed from beneath, so that he may be represented
as a sacrifice to Odin. Thus rather than belonging
to the human world, these young warriors whose
helmets bear horns ending in eagles' beaks, the
mark of Odin, could be the *einherjar*, the special
champions of the god from the Other World,
acting as his faithful and courageous emissaries
on the battlefield, as they are said to do in the
Edda poems.

The berserks

Snorri tells us that the warriors of Odin fought
in an inspired frenzy, trusting in the power of
the god to deliver them from wounds, and that
such warriors were known as berserks. They
wore the skins of bears or wolves, and they
howled like beasts when the battle madness came
upon them. Such redoutable fighters are said to
have formed the bodyguard of the heathen kings
of Norway. Berserks may appear rather like
fairy-tale ogres in the later literature, but there

is reason to believe that in the Migration period they were a privileged company of dedicated warriors, who devoted their lives to fighting, and were fed and supported by the community as followers of the god. The semi-human figures resembling bears and wolves and carrying weapons, which appear on the helmet plates, may represent the berserks. There are ruthless figures of dedicated warriors in many of Saxo's stories, reproaching kings for their cowardice, taking merciless vengeance, and challenging other champions or monsters to battle. Not surprisingly, they seem to have been somewhat unpopular figures, but it may well have been men of this kind who kept the cult of Odin alive and helped to preserve the rich body of traditions about ancient heroes which has come down to us.

Some of the stories of the supernatural in the sagas may be better understood if we see them as based on the lore of such warrior companies. When for instance Sigmund the Volsung and Sinfjotli his son took to the woods to escape

their enemies, they are said to have put on wolf-skins and to have used the speech of wolves. Their behaviour was governed by the law of the wolf-pack and they howled when attacked. They undertook to take on as many as seven men at once, but no more. Bodvar *biarki*, the famous warrior of the Danish king Hrolf *kraki*, is said to have gone out to fight in the likeness of a great bear, against which the enemy were powerless, while the warrior himself remained at home and seemed to sleep. The practices of the followers of Odin, fighting like wild beasts in a state of ecstasy which allowed escape for a while from self-consciousness and made them impervious to pain and fear, are reflected in such stories of shape-changing by warriors, dimly remembered and written down long after the berserks had vanished from the scene.

Right: a mount in bronze in the form of a bird mask, probably from the top of a staff. Late Bronze Age. National Historical Museum, Stockholm.

Below: a small bronze figure of a woman with eyes of gold found with a serpent and three animal heads which resemble the bird-like horses of the rock carvings. They were found at Fardal in Lapland and belong to the late Bronze Age. The woman's posture suggests that she is driving, and the serpent and animal heads may have formed part of her equipage. Her necklace, plait of hair and left hand grasping her breast suggest that she represents the goddess of fertility. National Museum, Copenhagen.

Wolf, eagle and raven

It was not only the little naked warriors who represented the influence of Odin on the field of battle. The wolf was linked with the berserks and closely associated with the god, who was said to keep two wolves beside him which he fed when he presided over the feasting in Valhalla. Wolves were constantly introduced into accounts of battles in heroic poetry, and were said to meet with the eagles and ravens who came to feast upon the slain. These birds of the battlefield were also used as symbols of the god. The eagle no doubt owed something to its use as a Roman symbol for the Emperor, but it was adopted by the Germanic peoples as a powerful religious symbol of their own, and was known also to the Celts. Warriors wearing helmets with eagle crests appear on Vendel helmet plates, and there are splendid eagles on the great royal shield from Sutton Hoo. Eagle brooches were found in large quantities throughout the Germanic world, some of them elaborate and richly ornamented. On Gotland stones of the Viking Age the eagle appears frequently, presiding over scenes of battle and sacrifice, and in one scene welcomed by a woman with a horn, as if entering Valhalla. The raven also is shown on the Vendel helmet plates flying with the eagle beside the mounted warrior who may represent Odin himself. The god was said to possess two ravens whom he sent out far and wide to bring him tidings, and whose names appear to mean Thought and Memory. They may symbolise the sending out of his spirit into other worlds. The sight of a raven was held to be a good omen

to a worshipper of the god, and there are tales of raven banners possessing magical powers, which brought good fortune and overwhelming victory in battle.

The valkyries

All these creatures were viewed at times as the messengers of Odin, but later the chief emphasis was placed on his warrior maidens, the valkyries. These, like the ravens and the *einherjar*, were said to be choosers of the slain. They seem originally to have been fierce female spirits attendant on the war-god, delighting in blood and carnage and devouring corpses on the battlefield. Later in the Viking Age they developed into more dignified figures, princesses riding in armour on horseback. They escorted the royal

themselves to the kings and princes who worshipped Odin, giving them help and counsel and bringing them luck in battle, while at death they received them as their 'husbands'.

One of the most famous of such valkyries was Brynhild, the heroine of the story of Sigurd the Volsung. She dared to disobey the commands of Odin, and gave victory to a king whom the god had condemned to death. As a punishment for this, she was placed by Odin within a wall of fire, where she lay in an enchanted sleep, until Sigurd on his wonderful horse Grani, a gift from Odin, rode through the flames and awakened her, to play a new and tragic part in the story of yet another of Odin's heroes.

Brynhild in the story as we have it appears in a double role, both as supernatural valkyrie

Dies used for making helmet plates, found at Torslunda on the island of Öland in the Baltic. They date from the sixth century A.D. The figures were probably intended to bring luck in battle. The dancing youth in a horned helmet is believed to be a follower of Odin, possibly one of his messengers who decided the fate of warriors in battle. The human figure with an animal head may represent one of the berserks, said to change into wolves or bears in the fury of battle. The man with the axe holding a monster on a chain suggests the myth of Tyr binding the wolf.

warriors who died to Valhalla and there welcomed them with horns of mead, as they are seen doing on many of the Gotland stones. On some of these stones a female figure can also be seen flying with a spear above the scene of conflict. Little silver amulets of women bearing horns, like those on the stones, have been found in Swedish graves at Birka and elsewhere.

Valkyries play a great part in the stories and poems about the exploits of the legendary heroes. Sometimes they are described as powerful supernatural beings of giant stature, striding across the mountains or appearing in time of danger to take up the hero and to carry him out of his predicament. They are said by Saxo to vary their appearance, and to be seen sometimes as fearsome beings and sometimes as beautiful maidens, who offer love to the warrior. Protective spirits of this kind were said to attach

and human princess, and this is true of other valkyrie figures. Svava, the protector of the hero Helgi, was said to be reborn as Sigrun, the princess who married a later Helgi, and Sigrun is described in the poem as joining her dead husband within the grave mound. Indeed there is some implication that these valkyrie figures were attached as guardian spirits to certain families, and befriended warriors of succeeding generations, receiving them at death and then appearing again on earth to welcome their descendants and to support and strengthen them in turn.

Such maiden warriors are said to ride in companies. Swanwhite, for example, in Saxo's story befriended the young hero Ragnar, giving him a sword and urging him on to great deeds. She came to him riding with a troop of maidens, but was clearly not a being of this world, for she was at first enveloped in mist and darkness and then revealed herself as a woman of great beauty, who offered to become his betrothed. The Anglo-Saxons too had memories of such mighty women, for there is a spell which describes a band of them riding over the hill and flinging spears to cause disaster to their victims. A human figure with an animal head, seen confronting a warrior in an eagle helmet on the Franks Casket, a carved ivory box of the seventh century made in Northumbria, suggests a valkyrie in her terrible aspect meeting one of the warriors of Odin.

Valhalla in the grave

Odin was primarily the god of the dead and ruler of the underworld, and his hall, Valhalla, appears to have been a symbol of the grave rather than some bright abode of the sky. The account of Odin's hall as given by Snorri in the *Prose Edda*, from which most popular descriptions of Valhalla have been taken, is based almost entirely on one poem, *Grimnismál*. There it is said to be a hall with many doors, filled with shields and mailcoats and haunted by the wolf and the eagle. It seems indeed to be a kind of riddling account of the field of battle, where the wolf and eagle are busy, and where the doors of death are opened for many. At the same time it represents the grave where the dead rest, and where they are received by their ancestors with rejoicing. The banquet in the Other World was sometimes symbolised, as we have seen, by the furnishing of the grave. Much later in Iceland there is reference to a belief that the dead from certain families entered a sacred mountain, Holyfell, and there joined their kindred. Those who passed that way after a funeral might hear sounds

Head of the man discovered in a peat bog at Tollund, Denmark, who died in the Migration period by strangling. The rope was still in place round his neck.

of feasting and merriment as the dead man was welcomed within the hill.

The unceasing battle said to continue every day in Valhalla is also found in stories of the grave mound itself. One of Olaf Tryggvason's men was said to have broken into a huge tumulus, and to have found within twelve men in black and twelve in red, who fought continually. They could not slay their opponents, for those who were overthrown sprang up and continued the battle, and it was only the human visitant who was able to deal them wounds from which there was no recovery. An unceasing battle is also described as going on in the underworld realm of the dead to which a supernatural guide, perhaps a valkyrie, led the hero Hadding in a story told by Saxo. The most famous account of the everlasting conflict is that of Hedin and Hild, two lovers who were parted by the enmity between Hild's father and her lover. Hild, who bears the name, it may be noted, of a valkyrie, aroused the slain men on the field of battle every evening, so that in the morning they were able to resume the fight. It is possible that a scene associated with this story is shown on one of the Gotland stones, where a woman stands between two armies.

Women sacrificed to Odin

Sacrifices to Odin might include women as well as men. The wives or female slaves of high-born men in the Viking Age are represented as voluntarily giving themselves to death when their men died, and the implication is that by such sacrifice they won high honour in the Other World. One of the most moving of Saxo's stories is of two lovers, parted like Hedin and Hild by a family feud. The young man was captured when visiting his beloved and condemned to die by hanging. When she believed him to be dead, Signy and her maidens prepared to hang themselves in the hall, first setting the building alight so that their bodies would be burned. The hero, Hagbard, had delayed his death for a few moments, so that he caught sight of the rising flames.

He declared in a triumphant death-song that now their love would continue in the Other World, where they would be joined once more as they could not be in life. Similarly, although Brynhild was unable to marry Sigurd, who had awakened her from sleep and whom she regarded as her rightful husband, she had herself burned on a great funeral pyre when she learned that

he had been slain, so that she might join him as his wife. There is indication that voluntary sacrifice of this kind was regularly associated with the heroes of Odin and their loyal womenfolk.

Cremation and Odin

In these stories death by burning, as well as hanging and stabbing, is part of the sacrificial rite, and Snorri tells us that cremation was practised by the followers of Odin, who believed that the higher the smoke rose above the funeral pyre, the greater the honour in Valhalla of those who were received by the god. One famous sea-king, wounded almost to death in battle, was said to have sailed out to sea in a blazing ship rather than die in his bed. This story may be based on a tradition of cremation in a ship, for there is plenty of archaeological evidence for

One of the large Gotland memorial stones, from Klinte. At the top is a battle scene, a rider and a woman with a horn who may be a welcoming valkyrie. Below the usual ship and towering waves is a figure surrounded by serpents, and a scene which shows the defence of an enclosed place by an archer, while the man outside is accompanied by eagles. The tent-like structures probably represent buildings seen from the narrow end, with horns on the gables.

men being burned in their ships and the ashes buried in a mound, from the seventh century onwards.

From tenth-century Russia there is an eye-witness account by an Arab diplomat, Ibn Fadh-lan, of the burning of a Swedish chief in his ship at a Scandinavian settlement on the Volga. One of his slave women was put to death by strangling and stabbing in the traditional manner and laid beside the dead man. The girl consented to be sacrificed, we are told, because of the honour this would bring to her in the next world. She was feasted and feted for some time before the cremation ceremony, and before she died was held up before a kind of gateway built of wood. She killed a hen and flung it over the

gate, and then she looked over and declared that she could see her parents and kinsfolk seated on the other side, and her master surrounded by young men, calling to her to come to him. The killing of the girl took place within a tent on the ship. Two men twisted a cord round her neck, while an old Hunnish woman, called the 'Angel of Death', pierced her between the ribs with a dagger.

The symbolic act of throwing a dead bird over the gate is in agreement with the story of the visit of the hero Hadding to the Other World. The supernatural woman who was guiding him cut off the head of a cock and flung it over the wall that served as a barrier to the kingdom of the dead, and it could be heard to crow on the

Right: a memorial stone from Lärbro St. Hammers in Gotland. It shows at the top and bottom a death in battle and a ship which denotes the journey to the Other World. The centre panels include a meeting between two bands of warriors. A woman, possibly a valkyrie, stands between them. It has been suggested that she is Hild in the story of Hedin and Hogni, seeking to make peace between father and lover.

Centre: detail of the centre panel showing a warrior about to be hanged from a tree, the traditional method of sacrifice to Odin. The twisted knot associated with the god and the figure of an eagle confirm the link with Odin's cult. National Historical Museum, Stockholm.

other side. Thus in the tenth century we have evidence for ritual emphasising the feasting of the kindred of the dead in the Other World. The ritual was associated with sacrifice of a kind typical of the cult of Odin. In two graves of Viking chiefs in the British Isles, one in the Isle of Man and the other in Orkney, we now have archaeological evidence for the sacrifice of a woman at the funeral. The body of a woman was laid in each case over the grave of the dead man.

There is a constant emphasis on the willing-ness of Odin's worshippers to meet death, and the fierce delight which they showed as they submitted to the last ordeal. One of the great heroes of Odin, Ragnar Lodbrok, was said to have been put to death in a snakepit at the command of the king of Northumbria. We have a twelfth-century death song attributed to him, probably based on earlier poems, in which he concludes with the words: 'Laughing, I die'. When the ship on the Volga was burning, one of the men watching the fire declared to the Arab that they chose to burn their dead rather than bury them in the earth, so that they might reach Paradise the sooner. As a wind increased and fanned the flames, he added with a laugh that the dead man's lord, in his love for him, was sending a wind to take him away.

Sleipnir, the horse of Odin

In the Viking Age, Odin was pictured travelling through the air on Sleipnir, his mighty horse

the space of one winter. It was agreed that, if he could finish the work within the stipulated time, he should have the goddess Freyja and the sun and moon as payment. The gods thought themselves quite safe in making such a bargain, but the giant brought with him a marvellous horse, called Svadilfari, which was so intelligent and swift that when the beginning of spring was only three days away, the wall was practically complete.

The gods, however, were saved from making payment by the cunning of Loki, the trickster of Asgard, who took on the form of a mare and neighed at the stallion until he was lured away from his work. Thus the wall was never finished, and Thor slew the giant with his ham-

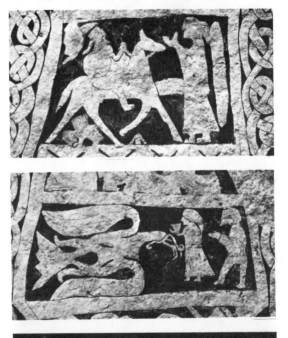

Two scenes from another stone from Lärbro St. Hammers (no. 3). Above: a warrior on horseback is received by a woman holding a horn. This is a favourite scene on the Gotland stones, and is thought to represent the welcome given to a dead warrior as he enters Valhalla. Below: an eagle is received by a woman with a horn. It has been suggested that this is Odin, returning to Valhalla after he has obtained the magic mead, or possibly being offered a drink from it by the daughter of the giant in the mountain.

with eight legs, which could carry him to the land of the dead and also bear the dead to his realm. The eight-legged horse is clearly portrayed on three of the Gotland stones, although he is not shown before the Viking Age. This may be a symbol originating in countries further east, for the eight-legged steed is recognised in parts of Siberia as the steed of the shaman, carrying his spirit to worlds beyond the earth. It is also used in India to describe the bier, carried by four men and therefore resembling a horse with eight legs, which takes the dead man to his funeral.

The story of the birth of this horse of Odin is found in the account of the building of the wall round Asgard, the stronghold of the gods. A giant offered to build the wall for them in

Top panel of a memorial stone from Alskog, Tjangvide, Gotland, showing a rider on an eight-legged steed which must be Sleipnir, the horse of Odin. Above is a flying figure with a spear, suggesting a valkyrie. The structure on the left may represent the hall of Odin, which is also the grave.

mer. After the meeting of the stallion and the mare, Loki gave birth to an eight-legged colt. This was Sleipnir, the finest of all steeds, whom Odin kept for his own. The wonderful horse Grani, given by Odin to Sigurd the Volsung, was said to be bred from Sleipnir and to be the best of horses in the world of men. Odin once carried the hero Hadding off on his horse, covering him with his mantle. They travelled over land and sea, and visited the hall of Odin, where Hadding drank from Odin's mead. Clearly Sleipnir could carry the living to the realm of the dead.

Odin in eagle form
Odin could also fly through the air in eagle form, and the eagle appears on many of the Gotland stones. The eagle which sat on the world tree may well have been Odin himself, since he had a special seat from which he could view all the worlds at once. Snorri tells us that Odin could lie as if asleep, while his spirit could journey in the twinkling of an eye to far-off lands in the form of bird or wild beast, fish or dragon. There are references to a bird and a fish in a long and complex runic inscription on a stone found at Eggjum, near Sogn Fiord in Norway,

which has been dated by some scholars as early as the sixth century. It has been suggested that these are references to Odin himself, journeying in spirit form as he comes to fetch the dead to the spirit world.

The winning of the mead
Odin flew in eagle shape when he won one of his greatest gifts to gods and men, the mead of inspiration. This mead was prepared from the blood of the wise giant Kvasir, who was created by the gods. He was killed by dwarfs, who mixed his blood with honey and brewed the marvellous drink. When the dwarfs also killed the father and mother of a giant, Suttung, he took vengeance on them by placing them on a rock and leaving them to drown. To ransom their lives, they had to give up the mead, and Suttung shut it up within a mountain. Odin set out to win it back for the gods, by a devious plan. He joined the men of Baugi, Suttung's brother, when they were working in the fields, and offered to sharpen their scythes with a wonderful whetstone. It was so efficient that they fought to possess it, and finally all nine were killed with their own sharp scythe-blades. Odin then offered to do the work of nine men in their place, if Baugi would in

return promise him a drink of his brother's mead. But when the time came Suttung would not agree, so Odin persuaded Baugi to bore a little hole into the mountain, and he crawled through this in the form of a serpent. He met Suttung's daughter inside, and stayed three nights with her, persuading her to let him take three drinks of the mead. In three draughts he emptied the three casks which held it, and then flew off to Asgard in the form of an eagle, pursued by the angry giant, also in eagle form. The gods had set out vessels to receive the mead, and Odin spat it out into them just in time, before Suttung could catch him.

Thus the drink of inspiration came into Odin's possession, and he allowed the gods and his followers to drink from it. It could give to him who drank the power to compose poetry, or to speak words of wisdom. An intoxicating drink was probably an essential part also of the ritual of sacrifice to Odin. We are told that the slave girl on the Volga was given a cup to drink before she was put to death, and that after she had finished it she seemed dazed and bewildered, not knowing what was happening to her. The arrival of Odin with the mead may be the subject which inspired one of the carvings on the Gotland

stones. Instead of the usual scene of a warrior arriving on horseback to be met by a woman with a horn, an eagle is shown in his place and the horn is held up to him.

Odin hanging on the tree

Learning and wisdom were held to be gifts from Odin. The most impressive of the myths concerning the god is that he hung for nine days and nights on the World Tree, even as his own victims used to hang, while he was pierced with a spear. He hung there as a sacrifice, 'myself given to myself', and fasted as he endured in agony, until at the end of the time he was able to bend down and lift up the magical runes which brought secret knowledge to men. This experience is described as if by Odin himself in the poem *Hávamál* (Words of the High One). Thus Odin underwent something which closely resembles the visionary experience of death and resurrection endured by the shamans of Siberia and elsewhere as part of their initiation, and as a necessary preliminary to achieving powers of prophecy.

To seek hidden knowledge, Odin also consulted the dead. In one of the poems of the Edda he is described as riding to the Other World,

Small silver and bronze-gilt amulets in the form of women, from graves of the Viking Age. Two hold up horns, like the women on the Gotland stones, and may represent valkyries. National Historical Museum, Stockholm.

down the road of the dead and past the fierce dog which guarded the gate, to consult a seeress, whom he called up from the grave to reveal the secret of the doom of Balder. It may indeed originally have been Odin himself who, under the name of Hermod, journeyed down the long dark road and over the bridge of the dead, in order to find a way to recall Balder from the underworld.

The one-eyed god

According to another myth, it was in his search for knowledge that Odin lost an eye. He gave this, according to one of the poems, as payment for a drink from the spring of Mimir, the spring beneath the root of the World Tree, whose water gave inspiration and knowledge of things to come. Another account of how Odin gained wisdom is that he kept the head of Mimir after it was cut off by the Vanir, preserved it with herbs and sang spells over it until it could speak with him and answer questions. He consulted it when he wished to learn the future.

The death of Balder

The myth of the death of Balder is essential to our understanding of Odin, since it enters into a number of the mythological poems. There is little indication of any cult connected with Balder himself, unless he represents the god of fertility under another name. Whether he was originally a deity or a legendary hero, one of the 'sons of Odin', is a debatable question. Balder was slain unwittingly by his brother, who according to Snorri was the blind god Hoder, but who in Saxo was another hero and follower of Odin. Snorri makes 'Balder the Beautiful' a god, and inhabitant of Asgard, beloved of Odin and his wife Frigg. Frigg, Balder's mother, had rendered her son impervious to wounds by taking pledges from all plants, trees and metals, so that weapons made from them would cause him no harm, but she neglected to ask one small plant which grows not on the ground but on an oak, the mistletoe. From this plant Loki made a dart and gave it to Balder's brother Hoder, suggesting that he should hurl it at Balder in sport. The gods liked to amuse themselves flinging weapons at Balder, since they knew that they could deal him no wound. When Hoder threw the mistletoe however, it pierced Balder like a spear, and he fell dead.

This calamity had been foretold to Odin by dreams and through his power to see the future.

He knew that it heralded the fall of Asgard. The gods held a great funeral for Balder, and he was burned on his ship along with his wife, who had died of grief, and his horse, like a true worshipper of Odin. The god in his grief laid his gold ring Draupnir on the pyre beside his son. Then Hermod rode down the long road to the kingdom of the dead, over a bridge whose guardian told him that Balder and a host of dead men had already passed that way, and finally into the hall of Hel, the ruler of the underworld. But Hel could not let Balder go unless all things on earth, living and dead, would weep for him. Hermod took this message back, and Frigg called on all created things to weep for Balder and bring him out of Hel. All might have been well had it not been for the resourceful Loki, who hated Balder and longed for the doom to fall. He turned himself into the likeness of an old woman and refused Frigg's request with scornful words, so that Balder remained among the dead.

This myth presents difficulties, for there is an obvious contradiction between Odin as ruler of the realm of the dead, to which Balder passed, and as ruler of Asgard, cut off from his son. The story must have changed with the years,

as is clear from the different versions known to Saxo and to Snorri, but the main implication is clear. Balder died against the will of Odin, the lord of death, in spite of all that could be done to prevent this, and the god could not release the youth he loved from the law of fate and mortality. This failure of Odin was irretrievably linked with the fall of the gods at Ragnarok. It was said that Odin went to great lengths and endured indignities in order to achieve vengeance for his son. This must have been an early myth, as there are references to it in one of the oldest skaldic fragments, but the story has survived only in Saxo.

The wooing of Rind

According to Saxo's version, it was foretold to Odin that he must beget a son to avenge Balder, and that this child must be born to Rind, daughter of the king of the Ruteni. He visited the king's court disguised as a smith, and proved so skilful a craftsman that the king gave him much gold to make into ornaments. Odin gave rings made out of this gold to the princess, who accepted his presents but repulsed him as a wooer. He proved his prowess as a warrior, but she still rejected him. He then touched her with a piece

Two small amulets from Sweden in the form of a man in a horned helmet, one in bronze with a sword and two spears from Ekhammar, Uppland, and the other in silver with a sword and rod (?) from Birka. The bronze figure came from a woman's grave. National Historical Museum, Stockholm.

Panel from a cross from Andreas, in the Isle of Man. Odin is about to be devoured by his ancient foe, the wolf. An eagle perches on his shoulder, and he holds a spear, turned downwards as if in sign of defeat. Manx Museum, Douglas.

of magic bark, presumably with runes upon it, and she fell into a frenzy. Odin appeared in the guise of a woman skilled in leechcraft, and so won access to the afflicted girl. Her father allowed him to bind her, and to give her a drugged drink. In this way he gained his will with her, and she was left bearing his child, while her father was overcome with remorse and shame. The son was Boe, who grew up to kill his father's slayer.

There are close resemblances between this tale and that of Weland the Smith, a supernatural hero, who in the same way tricked the daughter of the king who had made him a prisoner, and then flew away on bird's wings, leaving her to bear his child. The interest shown in this story, which is illustrated on the seventh-century Franks Casket and therefore was known to Anglo-Saxon Northumbria, might be more easily understood if it were indeed closely linked with the cult of Odin.

Traditions of Odin's cult

The confusions and contradictions in the tale of Balder's death illustrate the complexities of the myths about Odin which have come down to us. He plays a part in many stories of ancient heroes, a large number of which have been preserved by Saxo, but in a confused form, with many repetitions and contradictions. Such stories may well have formed part of the teaching of young men who were trained in Odin's cult, as princely leaders and skilled warriors. Scenes from such stories appear to have been carved on a number of the memorial stones of Gotland during the Viking Age, although many stories are now lost to us.

The traditions concerning Odin combine to give a picture of a somewhat sinister god. He uses cunning and duplicity to attain his ends, but he is forced to do so by the threat of fate and mortality against which he and his followers fight heroically but unavailingly. He is the leader of a lost cause, and also the god who offers to men intoxication to enable them to meet the worst that fate can offer without fear, and even with a fierce delight. Escape through excitement and ecstasy in one form or another was indeed the chief gift promised to Odin's worshippers. Yet in the Viking Age at least men had no delusions as to the extent of his power; they knew that he would always fail his followers in the end, because fate must prove stronger than he.

Small model of a bear and other animal shapes in amber from the mesolithic period in Denmark dating from before 2000 B.C. They may have been used as amulets or images of the sacred animals so important in the religion of the hunting peoples. National Museum, Copenhagen.

The god of the sky

Evidence from the Bronze Age suggests that the worship of a supreme god of the sky, whose weapon was the axe and whose power was manifested in the eternal round of the sun, was the predominant cult in Scandinavia a thousand years before Christ. After the Bronze Age no more ritual objects and figures of deities were left for us to find, perhaps because conditions had deteriorated and there was no longer leisure for elaborate ceremonial or religious art on the grand scale.

Symbols of the sky

Symbolic representations of the sun-disc continued to appear in the form of brooches and ornaments. In the rich Danish cemeteries of the first centuries A.D. the dead were given elaborate brooches based on the symbol of the moving disc, long associated with the god of the sky. In the fifth century a series of impressive stone monuments were raised in Gotland, with a huge whirling disc as the main motif, which was originally painted in bright colours. These monuments are found in association with other symbols of the Bronze Age, such as ships, horses with horns, and little men holding shields. On some of the smaller stones of the same period or a little later, ducks or geese as well as horses were shown beside the ship. These stones may have been inspired by new influences from the East. The symbol of the disc, representing the sun, is found occasionally on stones raised by Roman legionaries, but it is significant that the association of symbols follows an old familiar pattern, that of the cult of the sky god in the North.

The god Tyr

We are told of a god worshipped by the Germans whom the Romans equated with Mars. His Germanic name is thought to have been Tîwaz, and he was remembered in the Scandinavian pantheon as Tyr. Tîwaz received battle sacrifices, but he differed from Wodan, whose main gift was inspiration. While giving victory to his followers, he also gave to them the gifts of law and order, and he was regarded as the deity who upheld the universe. He ruled the realm of the sky as well as that of battle. Little is known of Tyr, except that men turned to him for help in war and put his initial, the runic sign for T, on weapons in the early Anglo-Saxon period. In the Edda poems it was remembered that his name might be used in this way to give help to warriors.

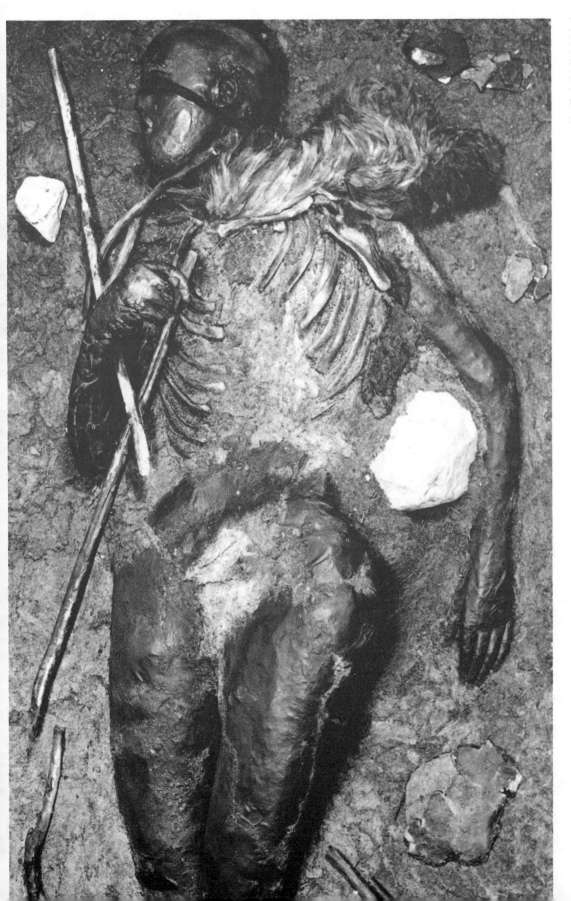

The body of a young girl
preserved in peat soil.
She has been blindfolded
and put to death by
strangling. This is one
of a large number of
bodies recovered from
the peat which may be
sacrificial victims of the
Roman period and later.
Schleswig-Holstein
Museum.

Elaborate purse lid from the
seventh century ship burial
at Sutton Hoo in Suffolk,
with a gold frame and
ornamental plaques of
considerable complexity,
decorated with garnet and
mosaic glass. The eagle
figure and the man between
two beasts are also found
in Scandinavian work of
the Vendel period, and
have associations with the
cult of Odin. British
Museum.

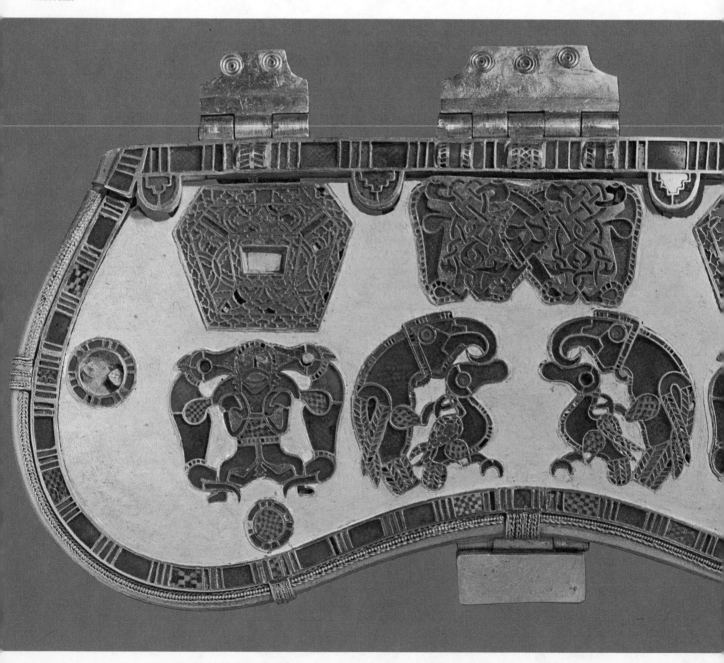

Small phallic bronze figure wearing a pointed cap, about 3 inches high, thought to represent the fertility deity Freyr, found at Rallinge, Södermanland, Sweden. National Historical Museum, Stockholm.

His importance is shown by the fact that one of the days of the week, Tuesday, was named after him by the Anglo-Saxons and Scandinavians, and a number of places also bore his name. It is possible that the lost hill figure of the Red Horse at Tysoe in Warwickshire, which appears originally to have been nearly an acre in extent and which was scoured by the local people every spring, had some connection with the cult of Tīw, the Anglo-Saxon equivalent of the Norse Tyr, after whom Tysoe was named. The god plays little part in the myths, however, with one important exception, the story of the binding of the wolf, when Tyr sacrificed his hand for the common good of the gods.

The binding of the wolf

The wolf Fenrir was one of the demonic offspring of Loki, and as he grew up in Asgard among the gods, he became so huge and fierce that only Tyr was willing to feed him. It was decided that he must be bound, and Odin in his wisdom caused the cunning dwarfs to forge a chain which could not be broken. It was made from the invisible and yet potent powers of the world, such as the roots of a mountain, the noise of a moving cat, the breath of a fish. When completed, this chain seemed to be no more than a silken cord, but the wolf refused to let it be laid upon him unless one of the gods would place a hand between his jaws as a pledge that it was harmless. Only Tyr was prepared to do this, and when the wolf found that the chain was unbreakable, the gods rejoiced, but Tyr lost his hand.

Fenrir was bound within sight of Asgard. He may probably be equated with the hound Garm, who guarded the entrance to the underworld, since this creature also was said to break free at Ragnarok and fight with Tyr. He may also be the wolf who pursued the sun, wishing to devour it. In that case, his binding was for the protection of the sun as well as of the gods, and for the maintenance of the cosmic order, upheld by the sky god. The myth of the loss of Tyr's hand appears to be one of the fundamental ones of the early Germanic world. It is thought by some to be represented on a few of the gold bracteates, amulets of the Migration period, where a male figure is placing a hand between the jaws of an animal. By the Viking Age, however, Tîwaz had been almost wholly forgotten, and his place seems to have been taken by Odin and Thor.

Above: bronze amulet in the form of a hammer from a sixth-century grave in the Anglo-Saxon cemetery at Ash, Kent. The circles may represent raindrops, and the loops at the top suggest a hammer on a long cord. This presumably represents the hammer of the thunder god. Liverpool Museum.

Right: small bone figure, 4.7 cm high, from Lund, Sweden, with staring eyes and a long plaited beard, which he grasps with both hands. It has been suggested that this represents the god Thor, and that the pattern of circles incised on the back of the figure is in the shape of his hammer.

Odin as sky god

For all his connections with the world of the dead, Odin seems to have possessed some of the characteristics of a sky god. He was called the All-Father, ruler of gods and men, and he was the adversary of the wolf, who watched jealously while he gathered his champions together. His symbols were the eagle and the raven, birds which could pass swiftly through the air, and he himself could travel high above the earth and look down from a high place into all worlds. The whirling disc would seem a fitting symbol for that intoxication and ecstasy which formed the essential characteristic of Odin's cult. The stones erected on the island of Gotland in the fifth century bearing this sign may, like the later memorial erected there in the Viking Age, be connected in some way with the followers of Odin.

A variation on the disc was the swastika, the hooked cross, used as a symbol in many parts of the world at different periods. It could symbolise a moving wheel and thus be a token of the sun and eternal round of the seasons. It is used on cremation urns from the Bronze Age onwards as if linked with fire. It is a major symbol on some of the splendid funeral urns of East Anglia, and it is likely that it was linked with the cult of Woden. We know from other symbols on the regalia in the royal grave at Sutton Hoo that he was worshipped by the East Anglian pagan

have attracted most devotion among the early settlers of Iceland in the ninth century. The heathen Anglo-Saxons worshipped him also and wore the hammer as a protective amulet. A number of places and a day of the week, Thursday, were named after him, as were also many Scandinavian men and women. In the late Viking Age the cult of Thor flourished up to the time of the conversion, and many myths about the god have survived.

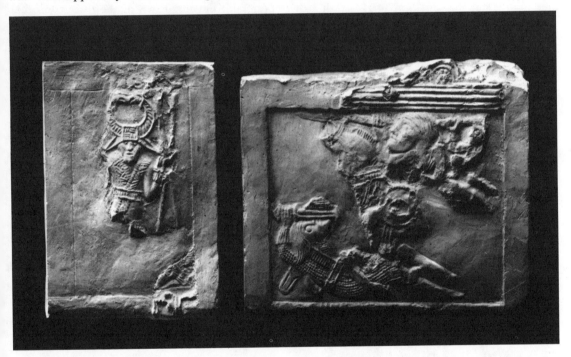

Two of the panels from the Sutton Hoo helmet. One shows a man in a horned helmet, originally one of a pair, and the other a small figure guiding the spear of a warrior on horseback. Other examples of both scenes are known from Sweden. British Museum.

kings. The swastika also appears on sword hilts and scabbards in Denmark and in Anglo-Saxon England, and appears to be used as a lucky and protective sign to bring victory from about the third century A.D. It was hardly surprising that the Nazis, seeking a revival of the cult of fanatical devotion to battle, chose the swastika as their badge.

The Germanic thunder god

There was, however, another god worshipped by the Germans who was associated with the sky. This was Thunor, who had power over the storm and lightning, and was equated with Jupiter by the Romans. His worship was said to have been conducted in forest clearings, and his symbols were the great oaks of central and western Europe, the axe and the hammer. As the influence of Odin waned, particularly in western Scandinavia, that of the thunder god, Thor, became of increasing importance. His cult seems to

The god Thor

In the myths Thor appears as a burly, red-headed man, immensely strong, with a huge appetite, blazing eyes and a beard, full of enormous vitality and power. He could increase his strength by wearing a special belt of might. Other prized possessions of his were his great gloves, enabling him to grasp and shatter rocks, the chariot drawn by goats which took him across the sky, and his hammer Mjollnir. This last was regarded as the greatest of all the treasures of Asgard, for Thor and his hammer formed a protection against the giants and the monsters, the enemies of gods and men. While Odin's main adversary was the wolf, that of Thor was the World Serpent, another of the terrible children of Loki, which lay curled round the inhabited earth in the depths of the sea, and would overwhelm the world if it came out against it, as it was to do at Ragnarok. The story of Thor's encounter with the serpent is told in a number of poems, some of them among the earliest we possess, and also in one of the poems of the Edda. But Snorri seems to have taken his rendering of the myth from another source.

Thor and the World Serpent

According to Snorri, Thor set out to visit the giant Hymir, disguised as a youth. Hymir was a sea-giant, and Thor offered to go fishing with him. The giant did not know that his visitor was a god, and he sent him off to fetch bait. Thor went to the giant's special herd of oxen, cut off the head of the largest beast, and took it back to the sea. Once Thor took the oars Hymir's boat moved so fast that he became alarmed lest they should come to the territory of the World Serpent, and indeed when Thor flung out the oxhead on his line, it was the serpent that took the bait. Thor exerted his divine strength and hauled the monster out of the water, until as he grew in might he pushed his feet through the bottom of the boat and stood upon the sea bottom. The terrible head of the serpent emerged from the waves to meet the fierce gaze

A stone from Hørdum Ty, Denmark, which shows Thor in a boat, fishing for the Midgard serpent.

of the god, but just as Thor raised his hammer to strike, the giant in terror cut the line, and so the serpent fell back into the deep. As the boat sank, Thor struck at Hymir in his wrath and then waded back to land.

In the longer account in the Edda poem, the story of the fishing is linked with the visit of Thor to the hall of a giant. He is said to have arrived there together with Tyr, and to have been befriended by Hymir's wife. When they had supper, Thor devoured two of the three oxen that had been prepared for them. When Hymir complained that there would be nothing in the house to eat, Thor offered to go fishing with him. There is no indication in this story that Hymir cut the line or that Thor knocked him into the sea. When they returned home, Hymir challenged Thor to break his most precious cup, which even when hurled against a pillar returned to the hand. Thor, however, was helped by the giant's wife. She told him to aim for Hymir's head, and the giant's skull broke the cup to fragments. Thor then took up the cauldron for which he had come, and which was to be used to brew ale for the gods, and strode out of the hall. A crowd of giants followed him, but he slew them with his hammer.

It seems likely that two separate tales have been joined together here, but certainly the account as Snorri gives it agrees with some illustrations of the myth found on three carved stones of the Viking Age, coming from widely separate areas. The clearest picture is on a stone now built into the wall of Gosforth church in Cumberland. It shows Thor with hammer upraised, and the giant beside him in the boat, while the oxhead is visible in the sea with fishes round it. The bait presumably has not yet been taken by the serpent, which is probably represented by the knotted coil that appears above the boat.

On a stone from Altuna, Sweden, Thor is alone in the boat, and holds the hammer aloft in one hand and the line in the other. The serpent appears to be taking the bait, and Thor has a foot protruding through the boat, as in Snorri's account. Another damaged stone from Hordum church in Denmark shows the serpent below the boat, although not much is left of him, and the giant seems to be about to cut the line, while again Thor's foot can be seen under the boat. The idea of the god putting forth his divine might, so that he became of giant stature and his feet reached the bottom of the sea, as

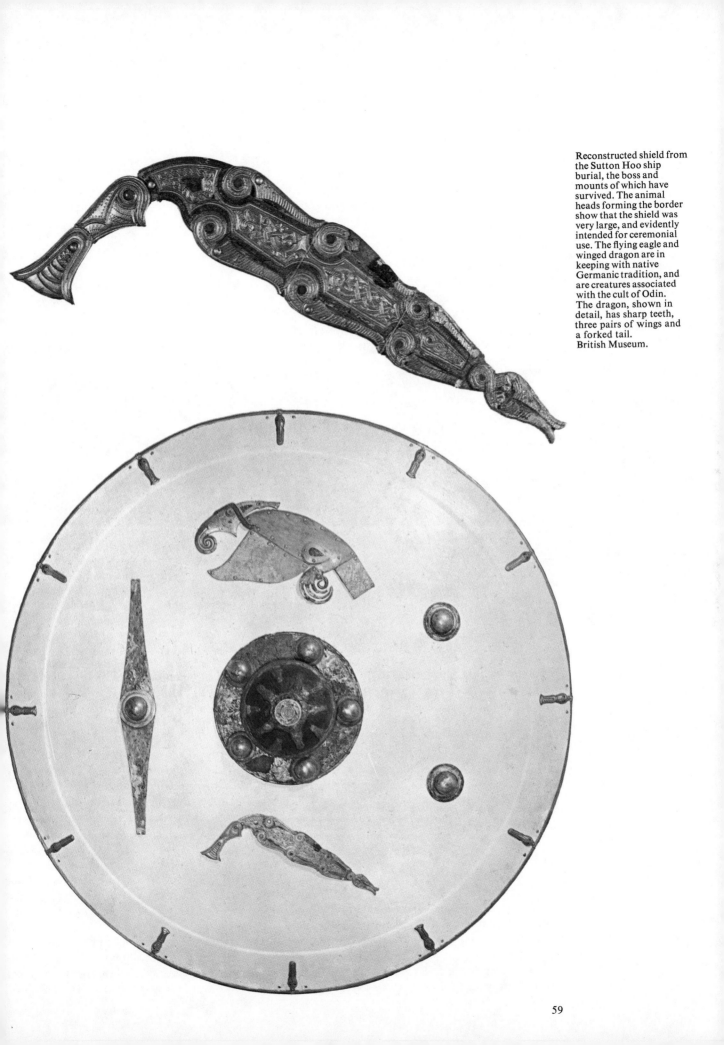

Reconstructed shield from the Sutton Hoo ship burial, the boss and mounts of which have survived. The animal heads forming the border show that the shield was very large, and evidently intended for ceremonial use. The flying eagle and winged dragon are in keeping with native Germanic tradition, and are creatures associated with the cult of Odin. The dragon, shown in detail, has sharp teeth, three pairs of wings and a forked tail.
British Museum.

in Snorri's account, is in keeping with other descriptions of Thor's exploits. The feet shown in the carvings are a significant feature.

None of the accounts make it clear whether the serpent was slain by Thor or merely escaped to the bottom again because of the interference of the giant, or, alternatively, whether it was trying to destroy the world but was beaten back. Snorri himself makes it clear that he does not know the end of the story. One possible implication of the myth is that Thor lost the opportunity of slaying the serpent when he was about to do so, and that this was a tragic failure,

of the late Viking Age. One story tells of Thor's duel with the giant Hrungnir, who had a race with Odin to see who possessed the faster horse and galloped so furiously that he found himself inside Asgard before he drew rein. The gods permitted him to drink from Thor's huge goblets, and the giant grew boastful, threatening to carry off the goddesses and to sink Asgard beneath the sea. Thor then entered in a fury, but the giant claimed a safe-conduct from Odin and challenged Thor to a duel.

It was a strange fight, as the giants set up a figure of clay, called Mist-Calf, with the heart of

Right: front panel from the box of carved whalebone known as the Franks Casket. The original of the panel is in Florence, while the rest of the box is in the British Museum. This panel shows a warrior encountering an animal-headed figure, and a horse and woman beside a burial mound, with other symbols which suggest a link with the cult of Woden.

Centre: helmet plate from the cemetery at Vendel, Sweden, showing a rider in an eagle-crested helmet, accompanied by eagle and raven, who is thought to be the god Odin.

resulting in the destruction of the world at Ragnarok. Certainly the fact that these carvings and a number of poems on the fishing exploit of the god have survived implies that this was one of the major myths concerning Thor, and it is possible that in an earlier version the sky god killed the serpent, as in other mythologies. One of Thor's titles is Sole Slayer of the Serpent, and such a myth would be in keeping with the pattern of a dragon overcome by the sky god which is found elsewhere.

Thor's duel

The rest of the story of Hymir as told in the Edda poem resembles other myths about Thor's visits to giantland, and his encounter with various frost-giants and their families. One early poem gives a considerable list of such exploits, but unfortunately most of the tales referred to are now lost. Snorri, however, has retold a few of them with a robust humour characteristic

a mare, to support their champion, while Thor was supported by his follower Thjalfi. Hrungnir the giant had a head and heart of stone, and was armed with a stone shield and whetstone. Thjalfi however advised him to stand on his shield in case Thor attacked him from below. He was thus unprotected when Thor rushed down upon him with thunder and lightning and hurled his hammer at the giant, who threw his whetstone in return. The weapons met in midair, and the hammer shattered the whetstone, before hitting Hrungnir's head and breaking it in pieces, while Thjalfi easily overturned the wretched Mist-Calf. The battle was now over, but the giant had fallen upon Thor, pinning his leg, and a piece of the whetstone had lodged in the head of the god.

Thor's little son Magni pulled the giant away from his father, receiving the giant's horse as a reward, and a seeress was brought to sing spells which would remove the stone from Thor's head. Thor however told her the story of how he had rescued her husband Aurvandil from giantland in a basket—another lost story—and how when Aurvandil's toe had frozen he had flung it up into the sky to become the star of that name. She was so interested that her spell was left unfinished, and the whetstone, according to Snorri, remained in Thor's head.

It has been suggested that this strange story is based on a ritual of some kind, in which a clay figure representing a giant was set up to be overthrown, perhaps as part of an initiation rite. The thunder god worshipped by the

Lapps before their conversion, who has clear links with Thor, was said to have a nail in his head and a piece of flint, so that fire could be kindled from his image, a fitting symbol for lightning. The connection of a whetstone with both Thor and Odin, who used one in his scheme to win back the mead from the giants, may perhaps explain the impressive whetstone, thought to be a royal sceptre, found in the grave at Sutton Hoo. This bears eight bearded and dignified faces, such as might represent ancestral gods linked with the royal house. Certainly the tale of Thor's fantastic duel, if only on account of the primitive form of the story, suggests an early myth, in keeping with other tales of the god in his position as warder of Asgard against the enemies of the gods.

Thor's visit to Geirrod

Thor often went out to encounter perils in the land of the giants. One tale describes his visit

Memorial stone found during the restoration of a church at Sanda in Gotland. It dates from about A.D. 500, and has a whirling disc with a dragon above and two smaller discs with serpent heads below. The tree below these is the only example yet found on stones of this period. The ship with rowers is an early example of a symbol which became very popular on Gotland stones of the Viking age. Visby Museum.

Rock-engraving of the
Bronze Age, at the edge
of the sea at Namforsen,
in northern Sweden,
illustrating the close link
which has always existed
in Scandinavia between
the gods of fertility and
the fruitful sea.

to the hall of the giant Geirrod. This was
brought about by Loki, who was captured by the
giant as he was journeying in hawk shape, and
only released when he swore to bring Thor to
Geirrod's hall without his belt or his hammer.
Loki succeded in this, by means not told to us,
but on the way Thor was warned by a giantess
called Grith, who lent him another belt and a
staff. This helped him to survive in the river
Vimur, which was rising in flood as he waded
through it, because one of the giant's daughters
was standing astride the stream, and it was from
her that the water came. Thor put forth his
divine strength, flung a boulder at the giantess,
and climbed out of the river with the help of a
rowan tree.

Thor and Loki went into the goatshed of
Geirrod, and there Thor sat down. But he
immediately felt himself being pushed up to the
roof, for now both daughters of Geirrod were
under the seat, forcing it upwards. He again had
to exert his divine strength and break their backs
before he could get free. Then he went into the
hall, where the giant called on him to join in
their sport, which consisted in hurling about a
red-hot bolt of iron. Geirrod took it up in the
tongs and flung it at Thor, but Thor caught it in
his gloves in mid-air and threw it back, and it
passed through a pillar and pierced the giant
through. This is the kind of game that was
played also in Hymir's hall, though there the
'ball' was a cup. Such stories are based on the
power of the thunder god to shatter rocks and
stones, a remarkable power which Thor shared
to some extent with his sworn foes, the frost
giants.

The recovery of Thor's hammer

One of the most vivid of the myths is told
humorously in one of the Edda poems. It
concerns Thor's encounter with another giant,
Thrym, who stole the hammer of the god and
hid it deep below the earth. Without the hammer
the gods had no protection against their enemies,
and Loki was sent out to search for it. He
returned with the news that Thrym refused to
give it back unless the gods sent him Freyja
for his bride. There was great consternation in
Asgard, and Freyja was so angry that she shattered her necklace in her fury. Then the wise
Heimdall thought of a plan, by which Thor
should go to giantland covered in a bridal veil
in place of Freyja, and Loki should go with him
as his handmaid. When the giants received the

veiled figure they took to be Freyja, there was great rejoicing, and a splendid bridal feast was held.

The giant was surprised by the enormous appetite of his bride, who devoured several oxen and salmon at a sitting, but Loki accounted for this by a tactful story that Freyja had fasted and gone without sleep for nine days and nights in her longing for her marriage. This also explained the terrible blazing eyes which the giant glimpsed through the veil. The giants were satisfied, and prepared for the marriage ceremony. That was the moment for which Thor had been waiting, for the hammer was brought in according to custom and laid in the lap of the bride. Once Thor had his hands on it, all was well. He slew the giant, his family, and the guests without more ado, and returned with Loki in triumph to Asgard.

Thor's visit to Utgard-Loki

There is another long story of a visit made by Thor to the giants, told by Snorri in his *Prose Edda*. This reads like a parody of other myths, the god being discomfited and humbled, but nevertheless it is an illuminating tale in many ways. Thor and Loki and two young followers set off for giantland one day and travelled through a dense forest. At night they found a huge building with a wide opening along one side, and they decided to spend the night there. But then what they imagined to be an earthquake took place, and the whole building shook, until in terror they retreated into a small passage on the right and stayed there till morning, while Thor guarded them with his hammer. A great roaring could be heard at regular intervals outside all night through.

They went out when dawn came, and found

Right: stone axe from the neolithic period in Finland. The human head at the end suggests personification of the axe and an early symbol of the god of the sky. National Museum, Helsinki.

Centre left: runic stone from Laberg in Denmark, with a hammer sign above the inscription and another below, in the position usually occupied by a Christian cross.

an enormous giant lying asleep, whose snores had caused the roaring they had heard in the hall. Thor buckled on his belt, but at that moment the giant awoke, and he was so huge that Thor hesitated for once to use his hammer. The giant gave his name as Skrymir (Big Fellow), and casually picked up what they had taken for a hall, but now saw to be his glove. He invited them to journey along with him and to share provisions, putting their food into his own bag. His great strides took him far ahead of them, but that night they caught him up under an oak, and he told them to get the supper ready while he took a nap. Thor for all his strength could not undo the string that closed the bag. He grew so angry that he struck Skrymir on the head with his hammer, but the giant merely opened his eyes and asked mildly if that was a leaf which had dropped on his head.

So they went without supper, and that night Skrymir's thunderous snores again kept them awake, until Thor could bear it no longer, and struck the giant a second time. The only result was that Skrymir asked if an acorn had fallen on him from the tree above. At dawn Thor struck him a third blow, so mighty that the hammer sank into the giant's forehead, and at this Skrymir sat up and remarked that a bird must have let something drop on to his head. Then he got up and took leave of them, warning them to be careful when they arrived at Utgard, since there were plenty of men there far bigger than he was, and to their considerable relief he strode away.

When they came to Utgard, it was indeed so enormous that they were able to squeeze in through the bars of its mighty gate. The king, Utgard-Loki, did not give them a very flattering

Left: small bronze figure about 2½ inches high, found on a farm at Akureyri in Iceland. It represents Thor with his hammer and was probably made about A.D. 1000. National Museum, Reykjavik.

Centre right: side panel from a memorial stone at Altuna, Sweden, with a runic inscription stating that it was erected in memory of a father and brother burned by enemies in their hall. It shows Thor in a boat, holding his hammer and hauling on the line after the World Serpent has taken his ox-head bait.

welcome, but he asked them what special accomplishments they could display for the amusement of the company. There followed a series of trials of strength and skill in which Thor and his companions were hopelessly outstripped. Thjalfi was defeated in running, and Loki in an eating contest. Thor himself, who was a champion drinker, was given a huge horn which he thought he would empty easily, but after he had taken three draughts, it seemed to be almost as full as at the beginning. Then he was asked to lift the giant's gray cat up from the floor. This seemed a laughable task, but when he exerted all his strength, he could do no more than raise one of its paws off the ground. Finally he was called on to wrestle with an old woman. For all his mighty strength he was utterly unable

to move her, while she forced him down to his knees before the king stopped the fight.

The visitors were then well entertained, and next morning took leave of the giant. Once they were safely through the gates, he told them how they had been tricked and outwitted by skilful magic which made them see things otherwise than they were. Skrymir had been no other than Utgard-Loki himself, and the bag which Thor could not undo had been fastened with iron bands. The blows which Thor believed had fallen on the giant's head had gone into a mountain instead, and left three deep pits in it. The opponent of Loki in the eating contest had been none other than Fire, which consumes all things as no living creature can do, and Thjalfi's opponent in the race had been Thought, swifter

than any man in its flight. Thor's horn had had its tip in the sea, so that it could never be drained, and the huge amount he had swallowed had been sufficient to cause the tide to ebb. The grey cat was no other than his ancient enemy the World Serpent, and when he had almost raised it from the sea bottom by his strength, all the giants were overcome by terror. His last opponent in the wrestling match had been Old Age, which can overcome the strongest. When Thor learned the truth, he raised his hammer in fury, but the giant and his stronghold vanished.

This long story, told with wit and irony by Snorri, seems half satire and half allegory. It reveals a good deal, however, about the nature of the god and his opponents. Thor is stronger than the giants, and has enormous power over the

universe, but this power can be rendered useless by hostile cunning. It does not appear to be an attack on the god from a Christian standpoint, but rather a characteristic comment from the late Viking Age on the gods, who, for all their mighty strength, were not supreme. Fate, ruling from the underworld, was mightier still, and they had insufficient wisdom to overcome it. Thor is pitted against the realities of life: fire, thought, the relentless sea, old age, and the monster in the deep, and against these he can find no answer.

Thor's wagon and goats
In the myths of Thor's expeditions to giantland, he is said to walk and to wade through rivers. But when he crosses the heavens bringing the

Two elaborate brooches in swastika form from rich graves of the Roman Iron Age in Denmark. These appear to continue the symbolism of the turning wheel which in the Bronze Age was connected with the god of the sky. National Museum, Copenhagen.

Below: fragment of a
stone found under the
church at Gosforth,
Cumberland, now built
into the wall there. It
shows Thor, holding
his hammer and
accompanied by the
giant, fishing for the
World Serpent.

stormclouds with him, he drives a chariot drawn by two goats, the rattling of its wheels making itself heard across the sky. The chariot is mentioned in the early poems, and one of Thor's names is Driver. Evidently this conception is an early one, and may well be a development from the idea of the wagon of the sun in the Bronze Age. In one story Thor is said to have lodged

at a farm and killed his own goats for supper. Then after the meal he had all the bones collected on the goatskins, and raised his hammer over them, whereupon the goats stood up and were again alive. Unfortunately the farmer's son had disobeyed Thor's command, and broken one of the leg bones to extract the marrow, so that one animal was left lame. Thor was very angry, but when the farmer begged for mercy, he pardoned him on condition that his son and daughter, Thjalfi and Roskva, should come away with him.

This story may be based on established rules at sacrificial meals, such as we know were held in honour of the gods, when cattle as well as horses were slain. It throws some new light on the symbolism of the raised hammer which could call up the dead to renewed life. It also confirms its use as a symbol on a number of memorial stones to the dead raised in Scandina-

via in the ninth and tenth centuries. As late as the twelfth century it is found on one Danish stone at the head of an inscription, the position usually occupied by the Christian cross.

The symbol of the hammer

The hammer of Thor was indeed a far-reaching symbol. It was not only carved frequently on memorial stones, but it was evidently in use at weddings to 'hallow the bride', as we are told in the story of Thor's visit to Thrym. It was worn round the neck or on a bracelet as an amulet, and in the tenth century large quantities of such small hammers were made in Scandinavia, some in iron and bronze, but more elaborate models in silver. The finest examples show many of the characteristics of the god which we have discovered in the myths: staring eyes, since the blinding gaze of Thor typified the lightning; a beard, since the shaking of the god's beard was said to raise a storm; and sometimes the beaked head of an eagle, which Thor seems to have taken over from Odin as god of the sky.

There are also dragon or serpent heads on some of these hammers or on the chains from which they were suspended, symbolising Thor's battle with the World Serpent. The ring on which the hammer usually hung was itself a symbol of the god, since we hear of a large ring kept in his shrine. A priest wore it on his arm at times and oaths were sworn on it. Thor evidently inherited certain of the characteristics of the earlier sky god Tîwaz, who was the upholder of law and justice, and it is significant that the

Althing, the Law Assembly of heathen Iceland, opened on a Thursday, the day of Thor. Thor's hammer seems at times to be identified with the famous red beard of the god. One little figure of a seated man grasping a hammer, found in Iceland and dated to the tenth century, has the hammer growing out of his beard. It may be noted that several men described as enthusiastic worshippers of Thor and acting as his priests have names such as Skeggi or Mostrarskegg. *Skegg* is the Norse word for beard, and these names may perhaps be based not merely on the appearance of the priests but on their connection with the bearded god.

The making of the hammer

The hammer of Thor, Mjollnir, appears to have been visualised as a throwing weapon on a ring and a cord, since this is the form in which it is shown on the memorial stones. According to the myths, it had a short handle. Saxo states that the hammer was broken in a battle in which the gods took part, but Snorri tells another more

Centre: bronze brooch of Viking Age in the form of two animals on either side of a 'thunder-stone'. Such stones were associated with Thor.

Below: runic memorial stone. The band bearing the inscription forms the cord from which the hammer hangs.

elaborate myth to account for the shortness. Loki in one of his fits of mischief cut off the golden hair of Sif, Thor's wife, and Thor would have killed him had Loki not atoned for his crime by finding two cunning smiths among the dwarfs who made new hair for her from real gold. At the same time they forged two other treasures for the gods, a ship for Freyr and the spear Gungnir for Odin.

Then Loki found two other dwarfs and organised a competition, wagering his head that they could not outdo such marvellous craftsmanship. They set to work to forge a golden boar for Freyr, and the great gold ring, Draupnir, for Odin, although Loki tried to hinder their work by taking on the shape of a fly and stinging them as they worked in the smithy. The third treasure they made was the hammer of Thor, which would hit anything at which it was thrown and return to the thrower's hand. But because Loki stung one of the dwarfs on the eyelid at the moment when he was working the bellows, the hammer was left with its handle a little short. In spite of this it was declared by the gods to be the finest of all the treasures, because it was their defence against their enemies the giants.

Thus Loki lost his wager. The dwarfs were going to cut off his head, but when Loki argued that he had not wagered his neck and they had no right to touch this, they sewed up his lips instead. Most of the objects mentioned in this story, spear, ship, boar, ring and hammer, were the symbols of the gods, and existed in the form of amulets in the Viking Age. This probably explains Snorri's remark that Thor's hammer could become so small that it could be kept inside his shirt, and that Freyr's ship could be kept in a pouch. The golden hair of Sif, as in the Bronze Age, probably remained the symbol of the goddess, and was perhaps connected with the ripening corn.

The axe of Thor

The hammer is a variant of the axe, symbol of the thunder-bolt. Little axe amulets are known from very early times, and large and beautiful ceremonial axes, recalling those of the Bronze Age, were still laid in graves in the Viking period. The famous ornamented blade from Mammen, found in a man's grave from Denmark, has a bearded head on the blade, and is probably associated with the cult of Thor. Stone weapons from neolithic times, and fossils such as belemnites and echinoids (fossil sea-urchins) were known as thunder-stones, and continued to be preserved as lucky possessions and protection against lightning, fire and other calamities long after the end of the Viking Age. There is an example from Denmark of a brooch in the form of one of these fossil sea-urchins, flanked by two horned animals which suggest the goats of the thunder god. Saxo Grammaticus tells us that the noise of the thunder was imitated in Thor's temples in Sweden by striking on metal with a hammer. Such a ceremony might account for the association of great metal cauldrons with Thor in a number of myths.

Worship of Thor

There are several passages in the sagas describing temples of Thor. They are said to hold huge images of the god, a bowl on the altar to catch the sacrificial blood of slain animals, and the ring on which oaths were sworn. Images of Thor were said to be made in metal, showing Thor driving his chariot, and also in wood, of the god sitting on a chair like one little Icelandic figure. Up to the present time, however, no convincing archaeological evidence for special buildings used as temples has been found. The descriptions we have may be assumptions by Christian writers, based on their own churches and perhaps on small amulets which survived into later times. Scholars incline to the belief that ceremonies in honour of the gods were held mainly in the open air, while sacrificial banquets would take place in the houses of the chief worshippers.

The pillars of the house

It is possible that small wooden shrines were built to hold figures of the gods. Little trace of such shrines would be left for the archaeologists. As far as Thor is concerned, it seems probable that he was closely connected with the family dwelling itself. We are occasionally told in the sagas that his figure was carved on a pillar or a seat. It seems also that the high-seat pillars, the main pillars of the hall in between which the seats of honour were placed and where the head of the family and the chief guest would sit, were sacred to the god. They appear to have represented the guardian tree of the family house, which in turn was the symbol for the 'luck' of the family and its continuation, a symbol which has lived on in Scandinavia and Germany up to modern times. The hall of the

Cremation urn from the Anglo-Saxon cemetery at Lackford in Suffolk. A number of urns from this cemetery bear the sign of the swastika, but this is the largest and most impressive example. Museum of Archaeology and Ethnology, University of Cambridge.

Above: outline of the Red Horse of Tysoe, now destroyed, but reconstructed from a series of photographs taken from the air and from the ground. The great horse was approximately 250ft long and 200ft high. The work of reconstruction has been done by Graham Miller and Kenneth Carrdus.

in their old home in Norway. Sometimes they threw the pillars into the sea as they approached Iceland, so that the god himself might direct them where to land and decide where he wished his new dwelling to be. Thus it may well have been the hall itself, rather than any special temple building, which was hallowed to Thor, and which was the place where worshippers sought his counsel, as the sagas describe.

The effectiveness of carved seats and pillars sacred to the god may be judged by the carvings in the wooden medieval stave churches which survive in Norway. Memories of pagan symbolism seem to linger in the fearsome wooden heads carved on the walls, while the main pillars which take the weight of the building rise like the trunks of great trees to the high roof. On the continent oaks were said to be sacred to Jupiter, the Roman god of thunder who was the equivalent of Thor among the Germans. Early Christian missionaries sometimes cut these down when they were striving to convert them. As late as the sixth century the East Prussians, who remained heathen long after their German neighbours were converted, had sanctuaries in the oak forests with sacred springs and figures of the gods placed within the oak trees. In Iceland, however, there were no oak forests, nor ancient family halls. It would hardly be surprising if those who recorded the sagas thought of the places were Thor was once worshipped in terms of Christian churches.

Volsungs where the hero Sigmund was brought up was even said to have been built around a living tree, and it was beside this tree that Odin first appeared to Sigmund, and into its trunk that he plunged the sword that was destined for the hero.

Worshippers of Thor carried their high-seat pillars with them to Iceland, so that they might be used in their new halls, and with them went some of the earth from beneath the pillars

Thor and fertility

The cult of Thor was linked up with men's habitations and possessions, and with the well-being of the family and the community. This included the fruitfulness of the fields, and Thor, although pictured primarily as a storm god in the myths, was also concerned with fertility and with the preservation of the seasonal round. In our own times, little stone axes from the distant past have been used as fertility symbols and placed by the farmer in the holes made by the drill to receive the first seed of spring. Thor's marriage with Sif of the golden hair, about which we hear little in the myths, seems to be a memory of the ancient symbol of divine marriage between sky god and earth goddess, when he comes to earth in the thunderstorm and the storm brings the rain which makes the fields fertile. In this way Thor, as well as Odin, may be seen to continue the cult of the sky god which was known in the Bronze Age.

Far left below: two Thor's hammers from Sweden, one an obvious hammer shape on a ring, from Laby, Uppland, and the other an elaborate model from Kabbara in Scania with many symbolic features associated with the god, such as staring eyes, an eagle's beak, a stylised beard, and perhaps a reminiscence of the World Serpent in the curving patterns below.

Left: one of a pair of magnificent hinged gold clasps, such as might be used to hold a cloak at the shoulders, from the seventh century ship burial of Sutton Hoo. The decoration is in cloisonné and filigree work, and the design at either end of the clasps is formed of two linked boars with tusks and crested backs, while the spaces below are filled by bird and serpent shapes: these are all creatures associated with the deities of fertility in the North.

A small box of whalebone, known as the Franks Casket, which is believed to have been made in Northumbria at the close of the seventh century and is now in the British Museum. On the lid and sides are runic inscriptions and scenes from native mythological tradition as well as from classical and Christian sources. The front panel shows on one side Weland, the smith who took terrible vengeance on the king who captured and lamed him, with the princess who bore him a son, and on the other the Wise Men bringing gifts to the infant Christ. On the side is the discovery of Romulus and Remus with the wolves, and on the lid an unidentified scene thought to be from a heroic story, of an archer defending a house.

The deities of the earth

While Odin and Thor were counted among the family of the Aesir, the gods and goddesses who brought peace and plenty to men were known as the Vanir, deities who bore many different names. The god who stands out most prominently in the literature is called Freyr, a name meaning 'Lord'. His twin sister was Freyja, 'Lady', and their father was the god Njord. Freyr was said to have been worshipped by the Swedes at Uppsala in the late Viking Age, along with Thor and Odin, and to have been represented in the temple there by a phallic image. He was described as the god who dispensed peace and plenty to men, and who was invoked at marriages. We possess one tiny but powerfully modelled little phallic figure, found at Rällinge in Sweden, which is believed to be a representation of this god. There are indications that the ritual of the divine marriage formed part of the cult of Freyr, and Saxo refers to some kind of dramatic miming which took place at Uppsala in his honour. He himself, or perhaps the devotees of Odin, about whom Saxo seems to know a good deal, considered such practices degrading and unmanly.

The wooing of Gerd

The myth of Freyr's wooing of the maiden Gerd is preserved in one of the Edda poems, and also told by Snorri. Freyr one day climbed into the seat of Odin, from which he could see into all the worlds. Northwards, in the underworld, he caught sight of a beautiful maiden coming out of her father's hall. Her arms were so white that their radiance lit up air and sea, and Freyr was overcome by desire for her, and could neither eat nor sleep. He sent his servant Skirnir on a long and perilous journey to woo the maiden for him, giving him his own sword and a horse which could carry him to the underworld. Skirnir at length reached the hall of the giant Gymir who was the father of Gerd. She refused the golden apples of the gods and the precious ring Draupnir which he offered her, and he had to threaten her with the magic sword and with the wrath of the gods, before she finally consented to meet Freyr in a grove in nine nights' time, to become his bride. The poem ends with a cry of impatience from the god because the time of waiting seems so long.

The usual interpretation given to this myth is that it represents the wooing of the earth by the sky, resulting in a rich harvest. But it is certainly not a simple presentation of this idea,

DEAE

NEHALENNIAE
DACINVS LIFFIONIS
FILIV V S L M

Figure of a goddess
Nehalennia, depicted on
a stone of the Roman
period found under the
sand at her shrine at
Walcheren on the North
Sea coast. She has a dog
at her side and a basket
of apples. Her association
with apples and the sea
links her with some of
the goddesses in the
Scandinavian myths.
Rijksmuseum van
Oudheden, Leiden.

for the confrontation of Skirnir with Gerd is complicated with esoteric dialogue about magic and the land of the dead, and he threatens her with a second death with all its attendant horrors.

The radiance of Gerd which lights up air and sea, and the introduction of Skirnir, whose name means Bright One, and who is otherwise unknown, suggest that there is some connection with the journey of the sun over the sky and down into the underworld. It is possible that the

The dead king

There is a close link between Freyr and the dead kings of Sweden who continued to benefit their people after their deaths. Snorri tells us in the history of the Ynglings, the early Swedish kings at Uppsala, that it was Freyr who set up the holy place there where the temple stood, and where we know that the royal burial mounds of the fifth and sixth centuries formed a centre of power and sanctity. Because of the prosperity which Freyr had brought to the Swedes when

Sacrifical scene from the Gundestrup bowl, which shows warriors with helmet crests, one of them in the shape of a boar like later examples from Scandinavia. This splendid bowl, presumably used for ritual purposes, is thought to be of Celtic workmanship, but is important for our understanding of religion in Scandinavia in the Roman period. National Museum, Copenhagen.

ritual of the divine marriage was linked with the reappearance of the sun after the winter darkness, or with the spring solstice. Certainly, of all the gods it is Freyr who appears to be most closely linked with the sun, although he cannot be viewed as a sun god, as was once supposed. The nine nights of waiting imposed on him are referred to again as preceding the supposed marriage of Freyja to the giant Thrym, and may have been a regular part of the pattern of a marriage ceremony.

he ruled them, it is said that they worshipped him and took his name, calling themselves Ynglings after Yngvi-Freyr. His death was concealed from the people until a great howe, or burial mound, was ready to receive him, with a door and three holes in it, into which treasures were placed in the form of gold, silver and copper. These were the people's offerings for plenty, and for three years they brought them, thinking that Freyr still lived. When they learned that he was dead, they realised

The slaying of a bull, shown on the base of the Gundestrup bowl. Its position in the centre, surrounded by figures of deities and scenes of ritual, emphasises its importance. Two dogs are attacking the animal, and a third dog has apparently been killed, while a man is about to stab the bull from above. National Museum, Copenhagen.

Right: a one-handed man among a group of human and animal figures on the gold horn without runes from Gallehus in Denmark, thought to date from about A.D. 500. British Museum.

Below: replicas of the golden horns found at Gallehus, Denmark, in the eighteenth century, later stolen from the royal collection and melted down. They consisted of a number of rings ornamented with human and animal figures, apparently concerned with ceremonial, which fitted over an inner lining of gold. They may have been the treasures of some shrine, and dated from about A.D. 500. One horn had a runic inscription, indicating that the horns were Scandinavian work.

that he must be still helping them, as the seasons continued to be good, and they called him the god of the earth.

There was a similar tradition in Denmark of a king whose name, Frodi, could mean 'wise' or 'fruitful', or rather a series of kings bearing this name, according to Saxo. One of them, like Freyr, was associated with a time of great prosperity, and was carried round the land in a wagon after death. The people believed he still lived, until he was finally buried in a howe. Offerings were also made to a dead king in Norway, an ancestor of Olaf the Holy called Olaf 'Elf of Geirstad'. Before he died Olaf commanded that every man should take half a mark of silver into his burial mound, and he prophesied that if a famine came to the land men would sacrifice to him.

The door made in the burial mound of Freyr implies that it was possible to enter the mound of the dead king and perform rites there, as in the great megalithic tombs of the past, although the royal graves of the Migration period were not collective ones like those of neolithic times. We find a reference in Snorri's history of the kings to wooden men, presumably images of Freyr, taken from one of his mounds and sent from Sweden to Norway. A number of wooden

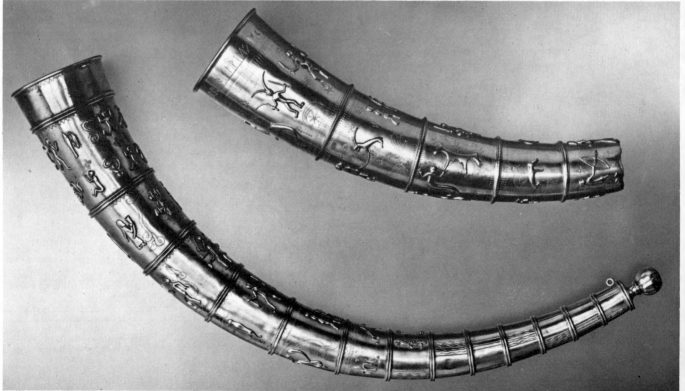

figures, some of them male phallic ones, from a period before the Viking Age, were preserved in the peat bogs. One from Jutland, a rough but powerful phallic symbol with a strangely dignified face, may represent a less sophisticated image of Freyr, the god of fecundity, than the little bronze man of the Viking Age.

The king from the sea
The god as worshipped in Sweden appears to represent a divine king of the past, a ruler in a distant golden age and the founder of the nation. Another figure of this type was known to the Anglo-Saxons as Scyld. He was said to have come to Denmark across the sea as a little child in a boat laden with treasures, and to have become their king, bringing them much prosperity. At his death, they laid his body in a ship, filled with weapons and the treasures of the nation, and sent it out to sea, so that it might carry their king back to the place from whence he came: such is the story told at the beginning of the epic poem *Beowulf*.

The story of a child coming over the sea to rule men and bringing them wealth and plenty was long remembered both by Anglo-Saxons and Scandinavians, and sometimes it was said that a sheaf of corn lay in the boat which brought the child to their land. Other similar gods of whom we know little include Ing, whose name was linked with Freyr when he was called Yngvi-Freyr and who was said to have travelled in a wagon over the sea, and Ull, who was said to have used a shield as a boat. They may have been divine ancestor-kings, after whom places and sometimes tribes were believed to have been named.

Wagon and ships
The idea of a fertility deity who travels in a wagon through the land after death, or over the sea in a boat, is a familiar image in the literature. He brings blessing to men, visiting them periodically, apparently as part of the seasonal ceremonies. This may be seen as a development of the myth of the wagon of the sun, of much importance in the Bronze Age, when both wagon and ship were potent symbols apparently used to represent the sun's journey across the sky and down into the underworld. As in Ancient Egypt, it seems as if the dead king in early times was associated with this

Head of a goddess, with attendants arranging her hair, from the great silver bowl found at Gundestrup in Denmark. This is one of the eight figures (one missing) round the outside of the bowl.

A fragment of the tapestry recovered from the Oseberg ship burial. The small covered wagon resembles those said to be used to bear the body of the fertility god or the king who represented him. University Historical Museum, Oslo.

Drawing of part of the reconstructed tapestry from the Oseberg Ship burial which shows mythological scenes and figures. In addition to abstract symbols, there are women who may be valkyries, and a man who seems to be hanging, suggesting connections with Odin and the cult of the dead. The tapestry was woven in a narrow band, about 20cm wide.

journey and with the blessing of his people, judging from the fragments of belief about the gods of the Vanir which have survived in myths.

We have also some archaeological evidence for the practice of carrying the god round the land. Beautiful and elaborate little wagons have been reconstructed from fragments found in the earth. Two were found at Dejbjerg in Denmark, broken in pieces and left, apparently as an offering, in a peat bog. They are thought to date from about the second century A.D. From a much later period we have a superbly carved wagon, whose carvings seem to have mythological significance, recovered from the Oseberg ship burial in Norway which took place at the close of the ninth century. This wagon formed part of the furnishing of an elaborate ship burial. Ships were used for funerals of both men and women and were buried in graves in seventh century East Anglia, and in Sweden and Norway up to the end of the Viking period.

It seems likely that such graves were prepared for worshippers of the Vanir. Freyr himself, according to Snorri, counted among his greatest treasures the ship *Skidbladnir*, said to be large enough to contain all the gods, and yet able to be folded up and kept in a pouch when not in use. The evidence suggests that ships were used both as offerings and also in processions in the Bronze Age. Examples of processional ships can be found well into the Middle Ages. The use of ships in carnivals, and the hanging of model ships in churches, sometimes taken out and carried in procession to bless the fields, has continued in Denmark and other northern countries into modern times.

The goddess Nerthus

At the beginning of the Christian era, the Roman historian Tacitus wrote a detailed account of the journey of the goddess Nerthus, known also as Mother Earth, when she travelled in a wagon round certain parts of Denmark. Her wagon was drawn by oxen and presumably held some symbol of the goddess, but only her priests were permitted to see inside. After her journey the wagon and its contents were cleansed in a sacred lake. The slaves who performed the rite were afterwards put to death, to preserve the sanctity of the deity. The wagon of Nerthus was welcomed with great rejoicing, and all fighting ceased throughout the land at the time of its appearance.

Freyr's progress

We hear also of an image of Freyr carried in a wagon in Sweden at the end of the Viking Age, although this is a late story and seems to have been told in order to poke fun at the credulous Swedes, who continued with such superstitions after Norway had been converted. According to the story, a young Norwegian who had fled to Sweden because of a disagreement with King Olaf Tryggvason, was invited by a priestess, called the 'wife' of the god Freyr, to accompany the wagon of the god on its autumn progress round the Swedish farms. She was an attractive young woman, and Gunnar was very willing to go, but when the wagon was stuck in an early snowstorm on a mountain road, Freyr himself came out in anger and attacked Gunnar. The hero appealed to the Christian god of King Olaf, and overthrew the heathen deity. He then put on the robes of the god and took his place when they visited the autumn feasts. The Swedes were most impressed to find that Freyr could eat and drink, and even, as subsequently became apparent, get his wife with child. They held this to be a splendid omen, and so increased their offerings to the god. At this point King Olaf, hearing what was going on, summoned Gunnar home, and he escaped taking with him his wife and child and carrying off a large amount of treasure.

The boar of Freyr

Freyr had another possession besides his ship. This was a golden boar, called Goldbristles, forged by the cunning dwarfs who made Sif's hair and Odin's ring. The description of this boar again bears some resemblance to the symbol of the sun travelling through the under-world, since he is said to have been able to outrun any steed, while the glowing bristles on his mane lit up the darkest night. The early Swedish kings treasured helmets with boars on them, perhaps resembling boar masks, which had names like 'Swine of Battle'. Warriors with boar crests on their helmets are pictured on helmet plates of the sixth century. An Anglo-Saxon helmet from a seventh-century burial mound in Derbyshire has a tiny bronze boar as a crest, with ruby eyes and gold studs on its body. Figures of boars were also stamped on a sword of about the seventh century, recovered from the river Ouse. Evidently the boar of Freyr could give luck and protection in battle as could the symbols of Odin.

The Oseberg funeral ship, shown in its mound at the time of its excavation in 1904. The burial chamber was built in the centre, and contained the remains of a woman, faint traces of a second woman, and some superb treasures in carved wood, which like the ship itself were preserved in the soil. The ship and its contents can be seen in the Ship Museum at Byggdøe near Oslo.

A splendid ceremonial
axehead from a man's
grave of the tenth century
at Mammen in Denmark.
The face with staring
eyes and beard at the top
is a method of representing
the thunder god. The
serpent on the blade was
associated with Thor.
Thor's symbol in the
Viking Age was both an
axe and a hammer.

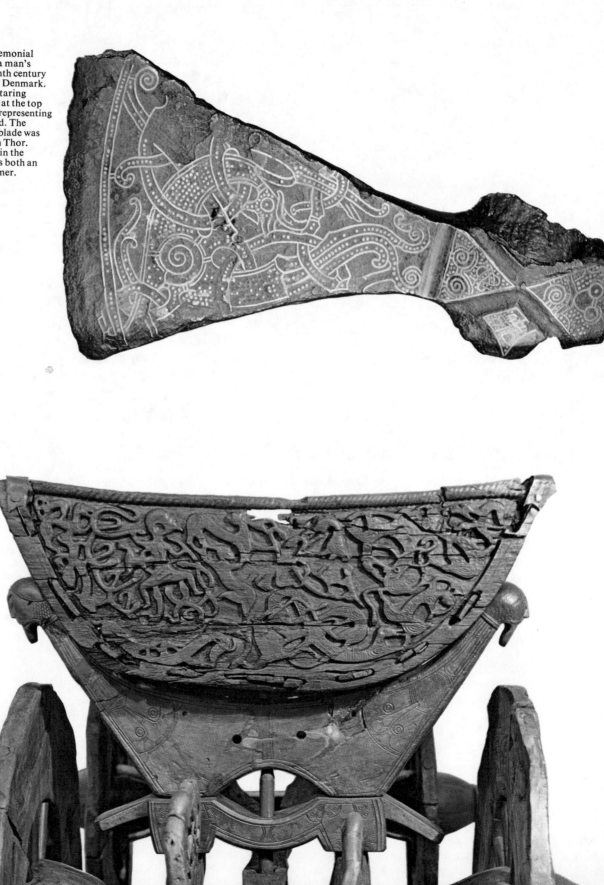

The sacred horse

There is a link between the horse and the cult of Freyr. The horse sacrifice, which was of great importance in the Migration period and later, may well have been linked with him. Particularly interesting is a tradition remembered in Iceland, that a stallion might be dedicated to the god Freyr by its owner, and that it was forbidden to any man to ride such an animal under pain of death. This is the theme of the saga of Hrafnkel, and in this story the horse dedicated to Freyr was kept with a stud of mares. There may have been a link between the cult of the god and the horse fights which remained popular in Scandinavia well into Christian times. They were held in spring in Norway and were believed to ensure good crops. A picture of two horses apparently being urged on to fight is shown on a memorial stone from Häggeby in Sweden, and there are descriptions of such fights in the sagas, although there they are not presented as a religious ritual. It is possible, however, that originally the victor of the fight was the animal that was chosen to be sacrificed.

What may be illustrations of scenes connected with the horse sacrifice were shown on one of the gold horns of the late fifth century from Gallehus in Denmark, beginning with the riding of a horse and ending with a priest or priestess carrying a horn. Certainly the importance of the horse cult is indicated by horse remains from Skedemosse on Öland and other cult sites in Sweden. There is now impressive evidence that the skull and feet of the horse were preserved, probably attached to the skin, while the rest of the animal was consumed at the sacrificial feast.

Snorri has an account of a feast known as the 'blood-offering' at the time of Hakon the Good, the first Christian king of Norway in the early tenth century. The king was forced against his will to take part in this. The people wished him to eat some of the horseflesh and to drink from the liquid in the cauldron in which the flesh was cooked, which would include the blood of the offering. At first he refused to do so, but compromised by opening his mouth over the steam from the meat. This did not satisfy the people, and next time he attended the feast, he consented to eat some of the liver. This sacrifice was evidently associated with prosperity and good seasons, and it was essential for the king himself to take a part in it.

The remains of horses are frequently found in graves, and particularly in the great ship-burials of Norway and Sweden and the Danish ship-burial at Ladby. A number of horses had been killed in each case and their bodies laid out in line in the ship or beside it, together with the corpses of other animals such as pigs, sheep, oxen and an occasional bird. There seems good reason to think that these were sacrifices to the Vanir.

Sacrifice to Freyr

Sacrifices to Freyr are mentioned in the literature, although no details are given about them. There is mention of a horse about to be sacrificed to him at his temple in Thrandheim. Sometimes an ox was said to be sacrificed, as in the saga of the hero Glum. Glum's enemy, a devout worshipper of Freyr, made such a sacrifice in order to gain the god's help, and got the desired result. Glum on the other hand aroused the hostility of Freyr when he shed blood on a field sacred to the god, which stood by the temple of Freyr and bore a name which has been interpreted as 'Certain Giver'. It was suggested by Frazer and others following him that early kings of Scandinavia were regularly sacrificed for the

Below: an elaborately decorated little wagon from the Oseberg ship burial of the late ninth century, in southern Norway. It is carved with scenes and patterns which appear to have religious significance, and is thought to have been used for religious processions. Far left below: one end of the wagon, showing a human figure surrounded by snakes and monsters. University Museum, Oslo.

The restored prow of the Oseberg ship, with its rich carving. It was hacked to pieces by the men who broke into the grave not long after the burial. They did deliberate damage such as would be inspired by fear and hatred of the dead within the grave.

good of the land and the prosperity of the people. Stories in the histories of the kings sometimes suggest something of the kind, for a number of them meet with strange and violent ends, and sometimes their wives are said to be responsible for bringing these upon them.

There is some evidence, as has been shown, that kings and members of the royal family were offered to Odin by hanging. But the possibility must be borne in mind that in Freyr's cult, as in Ancient Egypt, it was the natural death of the king, a time of crisis and danger, which was marked by elaborate rites connected with the god. Yet another possibility, for which there is evidence from Mesopotamia, is that the sacrifice of a substitute, and not the real king, took place at times of famine and peril.

The king on the mound

In any case, the accession of a new king was likely to be a time of special significance and impressive ceremonial. There is some evidence that the new king took his place upon the ancestral burial mound. Some mounds are built with flat tops, as though intended to be used as a platform for public ceremonies. Mounds of the Migration period sometimes had ancient standing stones or carved stone balls placed on them. The burial place of the kings at Uppsala was also the place of the local assembly. The mound at Tingwall, in the Isle of Man, is an example of this symbolism continuing into our times. It was built by Viking settlers over an ancient cemetery and has different levels, so that those of various ranks may occupy their correct positions, with the ruling monarch or his representative at the top.

Snorri has a strange tale of two local kings of Naumdale in the days of Harald Fairhair in the ninth century. They had been building a howe which took three years (the time associated with the building of Freyr's howe), but when they learned that Harald was advancing with an army, in his campaign to make himself ruler of a united Norway, one of the brothers retired voluntarily into the mound with eleven men, and had himself walled up there. His brother placed his high seat on the mound, in the place where kings would sit, and then rolled himself down to a lower position, that of the jarls. After this public surrender of his kingship, he came to terms with King Harald and was accepted as his jarl. There are indeed many scattered references in the literature to

kings and seers sitting on burial mounds, not only in order to make a claim to the title of a former king after his death, but also when they desired to seek inspiration. When sitting on a mound, they sometimes encountered supernatural powers or underwent some strange experience, and it seems to have been customary to seek help in this way from the wisdom and inspiration of the dead within the earth.

The king reborn

The power of the Vanir over the realm of the dead is associated with rebirth rather than with a journey to another world, as was the cult of Odin, although these two ideas are not necessarily opposed to one another. There is some implication that Freyr himself was reborn in the person of each king, while at the same time the king who died was identified with the god in the earth, and went to join his ancestors. Here again there is an interesting parallel with the ritual of kingship that prevailed in Ancient Egypt.

A tradition which persisted in spite of Christian disapproval was that Olaf the Holy, a Christian saint, was a reincarnation of an earlier Olaf, the Elf of Geirstad, who was buried in a

mound in Norway and to whom men are said to have made sacrifices. According to one story, the Christian king rode one day with his bodyguard near the mound of his namesake, and one of his men asked him if it were true that he had been buried there, and had once alluded to this as he passed the place. This made the king very angry, and he declared that his soul had never possessed two bodies, nor could it do so; he then galloped away from the mound as swiftly as he could.

The very fact that such a strange story has survived, however, supports the tradition. It was said that when Olaf the Holy was born, the birth proved most difficult, and not until a sword had been taken from the mound of the earlier king and the sword belt laid around the mother, was the child safely delivered. The ancestral sword was kept by Olaf's mother, and later passed on to the child when he was old enough to desire it. It was a symbol of the continuation of the line, and of the 'luck' of the earlier king being transferred to his namesake. The custom of naming after the dead, well attested from literary sources, was also linked with the importance of the ancestral tie and the continuation of the line.

A fight between horses, urged on by men at the side, on a memorial stone dated about A.D. 500 from Häggeby, Sweden. There is a ship on the other side. National Historical Museum, Stockholm.

The god Njord

The Vanir ruled not only the realm of the earth, but also that of the sea, which was an important source of life and food to a people depending largely on fishing for their livelihood. The father of Freyr was said to be the god Njord, who had close connections with both ships and the sea. His dwelling was Noatun, which means 'Enclosure of Ships', and he was said to give help in fishing and seafaring and to have power over winds and the sea. Places called after him suggest that he was worshipped down the Norwegian coast, as well as beside lakes and on islands.

Njord and Skadi

Njord was said to have married a giantess, Skadi, the daughter of the giant Thjazi, who stole the apples of youth from Asgard. When Thjazi was killed by the gods as he was trying to catch Loki, the gods agreed to allow his daughter to choose a husband from among them in compensation for her father's slaying, but she was allowed to see only the feet of the gods when she made her choice. She selected what seemed to her the handsomest pair of feet, thinking these must belong to Balder, but they were the feet of Njord. Skadi lived in the mountains, but Njord dwelt by the sea, and it was agreed that they should spend nine nights at each dwelling in turn. This arrangement, however, did not work out satisfactorily, for in a lost poem from which Snorri quotes Skadi complains bitterly of the screaming of seabirds which kept her awake, and Njord objects to the howling of wolves taking the place of the song of the swan. Skadi left Njord and returned to the mountains, where she went about with a bow and wore snowshoes. The myth behind this story has not been finally determined; one suggestion is that here we have a memory of two separate cults, and of some festival lasting nine days when a sacred 'marriage' took place, and one deity was carried to the shrine of the other. The problem is further complicated by the fact that the name of the god Njord is the male equivalent of Nerthus, known to Tacitus much earlier as a goddess worshipped in Denmark.

The Lord and Lady

The explanation may lie in the fact that the Vanir deities were always a male and female pair, a Lord and Lady, like the twins Freyr and Freyja. Nerthus was the goddess of the pair, while her male counterpart, Njord, was like Freyr a male god of plenty who came to be associated with water rather than the earth. His female counterpart had been forgotten by

the Viking Age or replaced by Skadi. Two impressive figures of more than human height, a naked man and woman, were found in a peat bog at Braak in Schleswig, and they could well be images of such a pair of deities. Another memory of them may survive in the tradition of the creation of Ask and Embla, the man and woman who founded the human race, created by the gods from trees on the seashore. It is vain to seek for a neat and logical mythology connected with the deities of the Vanir, who seem to have been worshipped under a multiplicity of names and to have been represented by many symbols. Behind these names and symbols however it is possible to recognise the form of the earth goddess of early times, whose cult centre was the megalithic tomb, and who was still a great power in the Viking Age, outliving, as Snorri put it, all the other gods.

The goddess Freyja

In the literature she is usually depicted as Freyja of the Vanir. She wore a famous ornament, the Brisingamen, which appears to have been a necklace, the ancient symbol of the goddess, although some have thought it may have been a girdle. In a late story included in one of the sagas of Olaf Tryggvason, Freyja persuaded the dwarfs to give her the necklace, and in return

for it agreed to sleep one night in turn with each of the four dwarfs who made it. Odin learned of this from Loki and sent him to steal the necklace. He found a way into Freyja's bower by taking on the form of a fly, and then, transforming himself into a flea, he bit Freyja on the cheek, so that she turned in her sleep and Loki was able to remove the necklace. According to this story, it was in order to get her necklace back from Odin that Freyja agreed to stir up strife between powerful kings, which resulted in the tragedy of Hedin and Hild.

Many places were called after Freyja, and she was said to be the most renowned of the goddesses. She was called the Bride of the Vanir, and was taunted at times for her unseemly behaviour and her readiness to take any god or supernatural being as a lover. She may have been regarded as the 'wife' of the early kings, as the goddess Thorgerd, who has close connections with Freyja, was looked on as the wife of Jarl Hakon of Halogaland who worshipped her. The valkyries who were regarded as the brides of the heroes may also have been connected with the cult of Freyja. She is said to have taken half the slain who fell in battle. Her name is linked with Odin as well as Freyr. In the story of the stealing of her necklace she appears as a valkyrie under the name of Gondul to prompt

Burial place of the Viking Age at Lindholm Hills, Nørresundby, Denmark. The two photographs show some of the 628 graves, 200 of which were marked by the outline of a ship in stones.

89

family, we are told that King Rerir and his wife longed for a child and prayed to Odin and Frigg. Frigg heard their prayers, and sent the daughter of Hrimnir the giant down to earth with an apple, which she dropped into the lap of the king as he sat on a mound. He shared it with the queen, who not long afterwards bore a son.

Another myth about the wife of Odin (here called Frija) has been preserved by an eighth century historian of the Lombards, Paul the Deacon, who took it from an earlier history. Frija called on her husband Wodan to give a

kings to battle. The giants also desired to marry Freyja, and the story of the recovery of Thor's hammer, when the god took her place and pretended to be a bride, depends for its humour on this. Sif, with her hair of gold, who was the wife of Thor, appears to be another manifestation of the same goddess. As always, the goddess was linked with earth and with the realm of the dead, and sometimes she appears in the form of the daughter of a giant from the underworld, like the maid Gerd who was wooed by Freyr.

The mother goddess

One aspect of this powerful figure is that of the mother goddess. Frigg, who is represented as the wife of Odin, seems to occupy this place, since she is queen of heaven. We hear comparatively little of her, however, and what we are told suggests that she too may be identified with Freyja. It is Frigg who tried to preserve Balder from harm and who wept at his death, leading all created things in lamentation. But Freyja also is called a weeping goddess, shedding tears of gold. Both Frigg and Freyja were called on by women in labour and were connected closely with the birth and naming of children. At the beginning of the saga of the Volsung

new name to the tribe of the Winniles, whom she favoured, and to grant them victory in battle. Wodan, who was supporting the Vandals, was unwilling to do this, and so Frija tricked him. She told the Winniles to come out at sunrise and to bring with them their wives with their long hair hanging over their faces. She then turned Wodan's bed round so that he would see them when he woke. His first words were: 'Who are these Longbeards?', and so the tribe of the Langobards or Lombards got their name, and with the granting of the name went the favour of Odin.

Idun and the apples of youth

Another mythological figure who seems to represent one aspect of the same goddess is Idun, a mysterious character said to be the wife of the god Bragi. Bragi is called the god of poetry, but may be no more than a doublet for Odin himself, since one of Odin's names is *Bragi*, 'leader'. Idun's function was to guard the golden apples of the gods, the apples which gave them eternal youth, and these, like the other treasures of Asgard, were coveted by the giants. One day when three of the gods, Odin, Loki and Hoenir, were travelling together, they attempted to roast an ox under an oak for their dinner, but the meat would not cook. An eagle sitting on the oak offered to cook it for them, if they would let him share their meal, but to their great indignation he took nearly the whole carcase. Loki attacked him with a stick, but the eagle retaliated by carrying off both stick and Loki through the air, and refused to let Loki go until he had promised to bring Idun and her apples into the land of the giants. When Loki returned to Asgard, he lured out Idun on some pretext, and the giant Thjazi, in his eagle form, swooped down and bore her away. Since the gods could no longer eat the apples of youth, they became wrinkled and grey. At last they discovered the part Loki had played in the theft, and threatened him with death if he did not bring Idun back.

Loki borrowed the falcon shape of Freyja, and flew off to the hall of the giant, where he found Idun alone. He changed her into a nut, and carried her away in his claws, but he was soon pursued by the eagle. As Loki flew into Asgard, the gods set fire to a heap of wood shavings ready by the wall. The fire singed Thjazi's wings so that he fell into Asgard and was slain. It was as compensation for his death that Thjazi's daughter Skadi was allowed to marry Njord.

Apples as a symbol of eternal youth and release from the tyranny of time are also found in Celtic legends of the gods, and the fruit has some connection with the kingdom of death. Apples were offered to Gerd if she would leave the underworld and wed Freyr. The expression 'apples of death' is used in an eleventh century poem in a context implying that apples are the food of the dead. Nuts are a recognised symbol of fertility, and both apples and nuts have been found in graves. In the Oseberg ship-burial there was not only a bucket of wild apples, but also nuts, seeds and wheat, all of which appear to be symbols of the goddesses of fertility. Another example of apples associated with a goddess of plenty was found at the shrine of the goddess Nehalennia, who was worshipped in the early centuries A.D. on the island of Walcheren in Frisia. Her shrine, covered by the sand, has been excavated to reveal a number of carved stones erected in her honour. Nehalennia was associated with the sea, and travellers invoked her help for a safe passage over to Britain. But she was also a goddess dispensing plenty, and in one carving she is shown with a bowl of what appear to be apples on the ground beside her.

The goddesses of plenty

There are many links between Freyja and the Mothers of the Roman period, those goddesses who dispensed gifts to men and who may be seen, usually as seated figures, on many altars of the Roman period in Germany, The Netherlands and Britain. Besides the goddess as a single figure, there are groups of goddesses mentioned in Norse literature. Such figures are connected with the giving of names, the presentation of gifts, and the blessing of children and young people. Saxo has a story of a king of the Danes who took his three-year-old son into the house of the gods to pray to three maidens sitting on three seats, who prophesied about the boy's future. Such figures are sometimes identified with the Norns, who decided the fates of men, and were said to dwell near the spring of fate from which Odin drank. They were called *Urd*, *Verdandi* and *Skuld*, Fate, Being and Necessity. There are also stories about groups of women whom Snorri associates with Freyja. They visited houses to bring good luck, and would foretell the future of children and sometimes hold divination ceremonies.

One of the names given to Freyja is Gefn, a name which must be connected with giving and also with that of the Danish giantess Gefion. There is a myth about how Gefion gave the Danish island of Zealand to her people. She was said to be the wife of Scyld or Sciold, one of the ancestor kings who brought the land prosperity. In her search for more territory she went to the king of the Swedes, Gylfi, who offered her as much land as she was able to plough. She visited a giant and had four sons by him, which she turned into huge oxen and with them ploughed round Zealand, separating it from the Swedish mainland so that it became an island. In this story the goddess may be seen in her character as a giver, and linked with the divine ruler of the golden age, the founder of the dynasty. She is also associated with the plough and with the fertility of the land. Two interesting traditions remembered about Freyr in the Icelandic sagas are that a field was associated with the god which was particularly fertile and had the name of 'Certain Giver', and that Freyr protected one of his worshippers from snow and frost after death, by keeping cold away from the mound where he was buried.

The symbols of Freyja

Both boar and horse were associated with Freyja as with Freyr. She is said to have permitted one of her lovers, the hero Ottar, to take the form of her golden boar and journey as her steed to the land of the dead, so that he might discover his ancestry from one of the wise giantesses of the Other World. Her boar is called not only Goldbristles, but also *Hildisvin*, Swine of Battle, the same name as that given to one of the great boar helmets said to be treasured by the Swedish kings. This suggests that a boar helmet or mask may have been worn by the king at divination ceremonies linked with Freyja's cult.

The most elaborate surviving example of a stone sphere, of the kind associated with burial mounds and graves in Sweden. This comes from Inglinge Howe in Småland, and is traditionally known as the throne of the king of Värend.

She is also associated with a mare. This connection seems to be a more sinister one, linked with the goddess in her terrible aspect and with the darker side of her cult.

Divination ceremonies

It was Freyja, according to Snorri, who originated the practice of *seidr*, the divination ceremony of which we hear a good deal in the literature. Either a man or woman might preside over this, but a *völva* or seeress generally took the leading part. Accounts of such ceremonies in the sagas bear a striking resemblance to eye-witness accounts of shamanistic rites taking place in recent times among the peoples of northern or central Asia. The seeress wore a special costume, of which the headdress seems to have formed the essential part. It was made of the furs of various animals, and sometimes included a pouch of charms and a cloak, while she carried a staff. Incantations were sung to invoke the spirits who revealed hidden things to her. She sat upon a special scaffold or high platform when conducting the ceremony, and seems to have passed into a trance. She was afterwards able to reveal knowledge of the future or of lost things, and to prophesy concerning the destiny of individuals, or give advice as to how a famine or dearth of fish might be brought to an end. Such visits from a seeress were mainly beneficial, to help the community, and thus in keeping with the goddess who gave gifts to men, but *seidr* could also be used for evil purposes, and was believed to cause injury or death. King Harald Fairhair was said to have put one of his sons to death, together with the band of wizards who supported him, for indulging in such practices.

It seems that the practice of divination was connected with both the god and goddess of the Vanir. In one story the king of the Swedes himself acted as priest, and consulted an unseen god in a wagon, although the deity in this case is called Lytir, perhaps another name for the male deity Freyr. Sometimes the seeress is seen in a mythological context, as when Odin rode to the land of the dead to learn Balder's fate, and forced a seeress to answer his questions, or when the poem about the creation and destruction of the world, *Völuspá*, is presented as the utterance of such a seeress. There seems reason to believe that both men and women, sometimes of royal rank, acted as interpreters and mediums who were able to prophesy through the cult of the Vanir.

The ship-graves

This may explain the use of a ship, the Vanir symbol, as a funeral offering in the graves of certain high-born women in Norway and Sweden in the Viking Age. In the Oseberg ship two women were buried, and there was a series of women's ship-graves at Tuna in Västmanland in Sweden, in what may have been an ancient cult centre associated with the goddess dating from long before the Viking Age. Not many ship-burials were made in Iceland, but two of those mentioned in the sagas were graves of men who were called priests of Freyr.

In the great ship-burials, remains of birds are found together with those of horses, horned

beasts and pigs. The goddess Freyja, like Odin, is said to have flown in bird form, and even on occasion to have lent her 'feather form' to others. This, as in the case of Odin, is a symbol for the journeying of the spirit, implied by the ecstatic trance of the seeress. It seems as if both the Lord and the Lady of the Vanir could be represented by men and women who acted as intermediaries, bringing their gifts of life, power and wisdom to men, and also those undesirable gifts of injury, sterility and death which rendered them feared as well as blessed. The Vanir are sometimes presented as giants and giantesses in the literature, because of their close connection with the underworld and the dead within the earth. There is some confusion between the Vanir and Odin, who was a god of the dead, and sometimes

represented as the husband of the goddess, while the valkyries who became the brides of warriors have some link with the goddesses who brought men gifts. There may indeed have been some rivalry between the devotees of the two cults, as is implied in some of Saxo's stories and also by the story of Viga-Glum in Iceland, when he appears to desert the cult of his family, that of Freyr, for the worship of Odin. It may also be reflected in the story of the war between the Aesir and the Vanir.

The cult of the Vanir invariably provoked most hostility from the Christian narrators of the old myths. It is often misrepresented or suppressed in the literature, yet probably of all the cults it has had the longest enduring influence after the end of paganism in the North.

Outline of a ship in stone at Klintehamn on the west coast of Gotland in the Baltic. This is one of the longest of the many impressive ships in stone from this island.

The family of the gods

When Snorri Sturluson came to write his account of the gods and goddesses, he pictured them as a company living together in Asgard, just as the poets of Ancient Greece placed their deities on Mount Olympus, in a community under the rule of Zeus. Snorri was led to do this by the picture given in the poems, where deities are related by marriage, groups of gods travel together, feasts are held in which all take part, and the gods attend an assembly like those of the Viking Age, to take counsel together and frame laws for the common good. Snorri placed Odin at the head of this community and made Thor and the other gods his sons, although it may be noticed that in his preface Thor is presented as the founder of the family of the gods coming north from Troy, and Odin as one of his descendants.

Odin and the gods whom Snorri calls his sons, apparently on the strength of Odin's title of All-Father and his leadership in the last battle, are known as the Aesir. The fertility gods, as we have seen, are known as the Vanir, and Njord is given as their head and Freyr and Freyja as his children. In one of the Edda poems, *Lokasenna*, or *The Taunts of Loki*, Loki makes attacks on the other gods and goddesses in turn, denigrating them with accusations of falsity, cowardice and infidelity, thereby throwing considerable light on the characters of the deities and alluding also to some myths now lost. Thus the picture of Asgard, like that of Olympus, is not a wholly idealised one, and quarrels and jealousies are by no means unknown, especially when trouble is deliberately stirred up by the mischief-making of Loki.

War of the Aesir and the Vanir

In particulars there is a tradition of an ancient war between the two groups of gods, the Aesir and the Vanir. This has reached us in a confused form, and Snorri tells two different myths about it, but does not tell us what was really the cause of the conflict. According to *Ynglinga Saga* Odin attacked the Vanir and harried their lands, and for a long time there was indecisive fighting until they grew weary of the struggle and gave hostages to one another. The Vanir sent their two leaders, Njord and his son Freyr, but the Aesir sent two gods of whom we know little, Hoenir, who was handsome but very silent, and Mimir, who was exceedingly wise. Hoenir was of little use in council, because he said so little, and the Vanir felt dissatisfied with the

Two panels from the doorway of the twelfth century church of Hylestad in Setesdal, Norway, showing scenes from the story of Sigurd. First at the bottom of the right panel comes the reforging of the broken sword of Sigurd's father by Regin the smith, then the slaying of the dragon, Regin's brother. On the left panel Sigurd roasts the heart of the dragon while the smith sleeps, and above is shown the killing of the smith after the birds on the tree have revealed his treachery to the hero. The top carving is from another part of the saga, and shows Sigurd's brother-in-law Gunnar in the snake-pit, playing the harp with his toes.

magic and the dead, which seems to have entered the North in the first centuries A.D. The gods Njord and Freyr, and presumably Freyja also, were reckoned henceforth to dwell with the Aesir and were accepted as part of the religion of Asgard, while their kinsfolk, the giants of earth and sea, remained in the underworld realm. This is a much over-simplified picture of a complex situation, but its general pattern is in agreement with the evidence which we possess of the history of religion in Scandinavia. On the other hand, there are parallels to the myth of a war of the gods in other mythologies, and this may well be a restatement of some earlier tradition.

Worship of the gods

While the outstanding deities, Odin, Thor and Freyr, had their separate cults, there was also regular worship of the gods as a group. Images of two or three of them are said to have been placed side by side in shrines and holy places, and at some of the great feasts of the year they seem to have been honoured as a company, in a community rite which was held independently of the individual cults. The man who

Above: a coffin formed from a hollowed oak trunk in position on its bed of stones within the burial mound at Egtved, Denmark. It contained a young woman dressed in a brown woollen jacket and short skirt, whose clothes and hair had been preserved intact, and also the cremated bones of a child.

exchange, so they cut off the head of Mimir and sent it to the Aesir. Odin preserved the head and used it for divination, consulting it when he needed wise counsel.

In another story in the *Prose Edda*, the truce was celebrated by a meeting of the two companies, and all the gods spat into a bowl, a recognised method of fermenting liquids among primitive peoples. From this divine essence a giant, Kvasir, was created, who could answer all questions. From his blood, after he had been killed by the dwarfs, was brewed the mead of inspiration. The name Kvasir comes from *kvas*, a word for strong beer still used in eastern Europe and for crushed fruit in Denmark, and Kvasir seems to be a personification of the intoxicating drink which could inspire men. Mimir on the other hand was a wise giant of the underworld, also said to guard the sacred spring of knowledge under the World Tree, from which Odin succeeded in obtaining a drink in return for the sacrifice of an eye.

The meaning behind the myth of the war may be a recognition of the rivalry between the two cults of the dead, that of the goddess of the underworld, which was known in the North from very early times, and that of Odin, god of

broke a solemn oath called down upon his head the wrath of all the gods, not merely that of Thor whose special province was the maintenance of law. We are told that figures of the three main gods were worshipped by the Swedes at Uppsala at the close of the heathen period, and these were the three deities whose cults have been discussed. One of the Arabs who visited the Scandinavian settlers on the River Volga in the tenth century describes how he saw a tall wooden figure with the face of a man, and smaller figures round it, to which men made prayers and offerings, although one figure in the group might be singled out by an individual worshipper for his special devotion.

Groups of deities

There are occasions when the gods are described as going out in groups of two or three. There is probably some specific reason for Snorri's group of three divine figures sitting on three high seats, one above the other, in the opening of the *Prose Edda*. He gives their names as High, Just-as-High, and Third, and it is they who reply to the questions of the inquisitive King Gylfi about the gods and their doings. The presentation of these figures does not suggest that they were an imitation of the Christian Trinity, and it seems probable that here as elsewhere Snorri was conscientiously basing his work on what he knew of pre-Christian sources. We are also told that three of the gods, Odin, Hoenir and Lodur, created mankind. Hoenir was the silent god said to be sent to the Vanir as a hostage. About Lodur we know virtually nothing. Some have tried to identify him with Loki, since Odin, Hoenir and Loki are said to travel together on other occasions. Thor was twice accompanied by Loki and once by Tyr in his journeys to giantland. When Loki taunted the other gods, they were all assembled at a feast in the hall of Aegir, god of the sea, and the company included many characters besides the main deities. Snorri tells us that there were twelve gods and as many goddesses in Asgard, but never made clear who was to be included in the list. Starkad, one of Odin's heroes, was once said to have witnessed an assembly of the gods, before the killing of King Vikar; it was held in a forest, and he saw twelve men there, while Odin, whom Starkad had known only as his foster-father, came to join them as the thirteenth member of the company.

Left: megalithic grave-chamber, known as King Gron's Howe, in a wood at Frejlevskov, Nystead, Denmark.

Above: a passage grave at Frøjlev in Lolland, Denmark, built of huge stones, with smaller ones to fill the gaps between them. The bones and skulls of many dead have been piled up in the grave chamber.

Left: the outline of a ship in stones, about 31 yards in length, at Gnisvere on the west coast of Gotland in the Baltic. This is one of the largest of the many impressive ships in stone from this island.

Below: helmet from Anglo-Saxon burial mound of the seventh century from Benty Grange, Derbyshire. It consists of an iron frame originally filled in by plates of horn with a figure of a boar as a crest. This is the only helmet with a boar crest found up to now although pictures of such helmets are known and there are descriptions of them in the Anglo-Saxon poem *Beowulf*.

Bottom: one of the great gold collars from the Migration period in Sweden, found at Möne, Västergötland. They were worn by kings, and are thought to be associated with the cult of Odin. National Historical Museum, Stockholm.

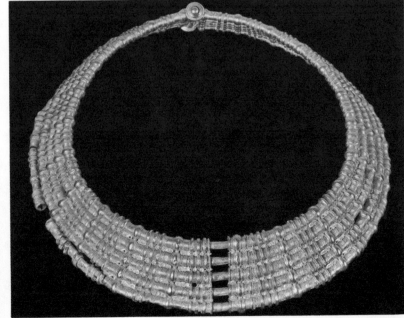

A number of bronze wind-instruments of this type known as *lurs* have been found in the peat bogs of Denmark, and some can still be played. They were evidently used for religious and ceremonial purposes, and are sometimes depicted in the rock carvings. National Museum, Copenhagen.

The character of Loki

A major part in the myths is played by Loki, who is introduced in the poem *Lokasenna* as the stirrer-up of mischief among the gods. A number of stories in which he appears have already been given. He helped the gods over the building of the wall round Asgard, luring away the giant's horse, and he also assisted Thor to win back his hammer, and recovered Idun and her apples from the giant Thjazi. On the other hand, he lured Thor into giantland without his hammer, and had helped to kidnap Idun. It is thus quite possible that he was responsible for the disappearance of Thor's hammer in the first place. In many cases he made atonement for his wicked deeds, and when he cut off Sif's hair he made this good by inspiring the dwarfs to shape wonderful treasures for Asgard. The main characteristic of Loki in these stories is not only his ability as a thief, thought by some scholars to be a very early feature of Northern mythology, but also the strange ambiguity of his attitude towards the gods. He seems to wish to help and hinder them at the same time, and even when the dwarfs were forging treasures at his prompting, he was seeking to spoil the work by tormenting them in the form of a fly.

The ransom for Otter

Another story in which Loki plays a major part is told by Snorri as a prologue to the saga of the hero Sigurd the Volsung. The gods Odin, Hoenir and Loki were once more travelling through the world, when near a waterfall they came upon an otter drowsily eating a salmon. Loki flung a stone at the otter and killed it, and bragged of his double catch of otter and salmon. But when they sought lodging for the night, they discovered that the otter had been the son of their host, Hreidmar, in animal form, and he and his other two sons bound the gods and refused to release them until they had paid compensation for the slaying. They demanded sufficient gold to fill the skin of the dead otter and to cover it completely, so that not even a whisker could be seen. Loki was sent to find the gold, and he captured a dwarf called Andvari and forced him to give up his treasure, including a gold ring which Andvari was most reluctant to surrender. Like Draupnir, this ring had the power to increase wealth, but Andvari declared that it would bring destruction on anyone who possessed it. When Loki took back the gold,

Odin was attracted by the ring, and would have kept it, but it had to be used to cover the otterskin, and so was left with Hreidmar.

The roasting of the dragon's heart

The curse did not take long to work, for Hreidmar's sons, Fafnir and Regin, killed their father to obtain the treasure. Fafnir then turned himself into a dragon and guarded the gold, refusing to share it with Regin. Regin went as a smith to the young hero Sigurd the Volsung, and persuaded him to kill the dragon, reforging the broken sword of Sigurd's father Sigmund which had been given by Odin. Regin counselled Sigurd to dig a pit and to stab Fafnir from beneath as the monster crawled down to the water to drink. Sigurd slew the dragon, and Regin then asked him to roast the heart, meaning to eat it himself. By chance Sigurd burned his thumb and put it into his mouth, and as the dragon's blood touched his tongue, he gained inspiration and was able to understand the speech of birds. On a tree above him sat two nuthatches, and these warned him against the treacherous Regin, who was plotting his death. Sigurd thereupon cut off the head of the smith, loaded the treasure on to his horse and rode away. The implication is that the possession of the ring of Andvari with the curse upon it brought misfortune and an early death to Sigurd at the hands of his wife's kinsmen.

The story of the killing of the dragon must have been an important one, since it has been illustrated on a number of carved stones from the Viking period in Lancashire, the Isle of Man and Sweden. Carved doorposts from medieval stave churches in Norway also show scenes from the tale. Although the style and treatment of the different carvings vary greatly, the same incidents are singled out: the stabbing of the dragon from below with a sword, the roasting of the heart and the thumb in the hero's mouth, the birds on the tree, the beheaded smith, and the horse loaded with treasure. A carved stone from Ramsey in the Isle of Man also shows Loki with arm raised to throw the stone, and the salmon eating a fish.

This story of the gaining of special powers through the eating of the dragon's heart has some of the characteristics of a myth rather than a heroic legend. It seems possible that the gaining of the dwarf's ring by Loki may be a variant of the tradition of the obtaining of the ring Draupnir, one of the treasures of Odin. A

ring worn by Odin's warriors as a sign of their dedication to the god of battle was indeed a possession likely to bring ultimate destruction upon the wearer. Andvari's ring in the end went back to Odin, since Sigurd gave it to the valkyrie Brynhild, and she wore it on the funeral pyre when she slew herself after the death of Sigurd. Draupnir is said to have been laid on the pyre of Balder by Odin, but it was brought back from the realm of Hel by Hermod when he followed Balder to the underworld.

The binding of Loki

The death of Balder is represented as caused by the evil plots of Loki, who indeed claims as much in a speech to Frigg in *Lokasenna*. Loki egged on the blind god Hoder to fling a shaft of mistletoe at Balder in sport, according to Snorri, although in Saxo's story Hoder is a human hero, the enemy of Balder, and he obtained a special sword called Mistletoe from the under-

Horned figure in bonds carved on a stone from the Viking Age found in the church at Kirkby Stephen in Westmoreland. It depicts either the bound giant Loki or the Christian devil. We do not know whether it formed part of a heathen memorial stone or a Christian cross, but the figure appears to be based on Scandinavian heathen tradition.

Far left: head of a monster carved in wood, one of five such heads in varying styles found in the Oseberg ship burial which are thought to have been carved by the same artists who carved the ornamented sledges. They have no obvious practical use, and were probably carried in procession or set up as symbols.

Left: a Christian memorial at Middleton, Yorkshire, showing the figure of a Viking warrior surrounded by his weapons and shield, as if representing the layout of his grave chamber in accordance with pagan tradition.

world in order to slay him. Loki finally prevented the return of Balder from the dead by assuming the shape of an ancient giantess and refusing to join in mourning for the dead son of Odin. Once the gods learned of Loki's treachery they sought vengeance on him. He fled from Asgard and built a hall with doors facing in all directions, so that he would see his pursuers approaching. When they came near, he changed himself into a fish in the river, but Kvasir, the wise giant, saw the outline of a net which Loki had burned on the hearth, and the gods reconstructed this and caught Loki by the tail at the third attempt. The gods then bound him across three flat stones, and left him with snakes dripping poison on his upturned face. His wife, Sigryn, brought a bowl to catch the poison drops, and it is only when she goes to empty it, we are told, that Loki writhes in anguish as the poison falls upon him, and causes earthquakes in the world. A scene carved on the cross at Gosforth, Cumberland, beside others which seem to portray gods and monsters, shows a kneeling female figure with a bowl beside another figure which may represent the bound Loki.

The giant of the Underworld

Thus beside the picture of Loki as the mischief-maker of Asgard, a nimble figure who is a swift traveller and can take on the form of bird, horse, fish or insect, we have another picture of Loki as a bound giant beneath the earth, a figure found in other mythologies. Loki has to some extent been identified with the Christian devil, and when we find a vigorous carving of a bound figure with horns on a cross-shaft from Kirby Stephen in Westmoreland, it is difficult to know whether it is meant for Loki or Satan. The figure of a bound giant whose struggles shook the earth was a powerful legend in the Caucasus region, and may have reached Scandinavia independently of Christian or Jewish tradition. References to a giant called Utgard-Loki, who lives outside the stronghold of Asgard, confirms this impression. This was the cunning king visited by Thor, who hoodwinked the god by deceptive magic, and he is also described by Saxo. When a man called Thorkill visited the land of the giants, he is said to have seen Geirrod and his daughters, killed by Thor in a previous encounter, and then to have visited the rock where Utgard-Loki lay, a huge giant laden with heavy chains. He was bound within a cavern, surrounded by serpents and loathsome

with corruption and decay. This is in agreement with the description of Loki as the creator of monsters, whose offspring were the great serpent, the wolf bound by Tyr, and the hideous goddess Hel, the ruler of the land of the dead.

Hel is used in the poems as a personification of death, but she might also be viewed as the female counterpart of the bound giant described in Saxo's story, for her characteristics are that she is half black and half flesh colour, terrible to look upon, and evidently represented as a rotting corpse. It is no doubt significant that Loki could take on both male and female form: he gave birth to Sleipnir in the form of a mare, and he appeared as an old woman when refusing to weep for Balder. The dead seeress called up by Odin in one of the Edda poems boasted that in reality she was the mother of three monsters, so that she must be Loki herself, prophesying the fate of Balder and the gods, and deceiving Odin just as Thor was deceived on his visit to Utgard-Loki.

The Trickster

The pattern into which Loki seems to fit best is that of the Trickster, a figure found in the myths and folklore of a number of North American tribes. There he takes an animal form, such as Rabbit or Crow. He may be regarded as a culture hero, since he brings benefits to mankind and sometimes seems to be a kind of parody of the supreme Creator god. Like Loki, he takes both male and female form, and gives birth to children. The semi-comic possibilities of this figure created folktales around him, as happened also with Loki. If Loki is seen as a kind of Odin figure in reverse, associated with death and the underworld, this may explain why he accompanies Odin on many occasions, and is said

in *Lokasenna* to have sworn oaths of brotherhood with him. There is also a confused tradition of a brother or rival to Odin, sometimes called Mit-Odin, who ruled for a while in his absence. Loki may originally have had a more dignified part to play than might be gathered from the comic tales about his mischief-making.

The god Heimdall

After the great gods and Loki, the figure among the inhabitants of Asgard who probably makes the greatest impression on the reader of Norse myths is Heimdall, the White God. He was said to sit beside the rainbow bridge to guard the entrance to the fortress of the gods from the giants and the monsters. He kept unwearying watch, since he needed less sleep than a bird, and his hearing was so keen that he could detect the sound of grass growing in the earth, or wool on a sheep's back. Heimdall carried the horn which would warn the gods when Ragnarok was at hand, sounding its blast through all the worlds.

His function as the warder of the gods links him with the World Tree, which was also the guardian of Asgard, but there have been many different interpretations of the traditions concerning him. One form of his name meant 'ram', and it has been suggested that he represented the offering of the sacred ram hanging on the tree, while the strange saying that a sword was the head of Heimdall could refer to the ram's sharp horns, its weapon of attack. On the other hand, Heimdall is also linked with the sea and the underworld. He was said to be the son of nine mothers, whose names suggest waves of the sea, and who are said to be the daughters of the sea god Aesir. He seems to have a special link with Loki, who is to be his opponent in the last

Left: tenth century cross in the churchyard at Halton in Lancashire. It has a number of scenes from the story of Sigurd the dragon-slayer, now unfortunately much worn, on the other side. The horse on the side panel is probably Sigurd's horse Grani, on which he loaded the treasure won from the dragon.

Above: memorials to the dead in the Bronze Age: burial mounds against the sky line at Fugile in Scania, Sweden.

Buckle of gilded bronze from the Anglo-Saxon cemetery of Finglesham in Kent, showing a naked male figure in a horned helmet and belt, with a spear in either hand. Institute of Archaeology, Oxford.

great battle, and there is also a confused tradition that Heimdall and Loki once fought in the form of seals for the necklace of Freyja. But this tradition survives only in a fragment of poetry difficult to interpret.

The visits of Rig

In one of the Edda poems Heimdall is identified with Rig, a name found nowhere else in the myths and presumably derived from the Celtic word for a king. Rig is said to walk up and down the land and to beget sons within the different social classes. He visited the house of the thrall, the farmer and finally the jarl, and in each was warmly welcomed by the householder and his wife, and lay down between them at night. Nine months after his visit a son was born, wholly typical of his own class. There are certain resemblances here to traditions in Celtic literature concerning a sea deity, Manannan mac Lir, and his son Mongan, since they were said to visit many houses to beget sons. It is possible that stories of this kind developed from memories of the duties of the king in pagan times; Harald Fairhair, for instance, the last great pagan ruler in Norway, was said to have had many wives, in different parts of the kingdom. He was expected to visit them in turn, and consequently he had a large number of sons.

Indeed most of the characteristics of Heimdall point to a connection with the Vanir rather than the Aesir, since he was looked on as the protector of the community and the father of men, while at the same time associated with the underworld and the sea. He fought for Freyja, to restore her treasure, and gave advice when the giant Thrym sought her in marriage. There are resemblances between his name and one of Freyja's many titles, *Mardoll*. Scholars have made many different conjectures to explain the cryptic references to Heimdall in prose and verse. He provides a good example of the difficulties of understanding the sources which preserve our northern myths.

Aegir and Ran

When Loki made his attacks on the gods, they were assembled for a feast in the hall of Aegir and Ran. Aegir seems to be a personification of the sea and its mighty strength, and his name is related to a word for water. The jaws of Aegir are said in the poems to close on ships. A fifth century letter by the Latin writer Sidonius describes sacrifices made to the sea by the seafar-

ers of the North, the Saxon pirates, who were accustomed to drown every tenth man among their captives so that they might be granted a good passage home. This seems to be a parallel practice to the sacrifices on land to the god of war. When dead sailors are said to feast with Aegir and Ran, and be welcomed by the goddess to their hall beneath the waves, there is an echo of the tradition of banquets in Valhalla in the hall of Odin. Ran was said to trap seafarers in her net, and if they had gold in their possession when they were drowned, they were sure of a good welcome in her hall. One saga also refers to a belief that if the ghosts of drowned men appeared at their funeral feast, this was a sign that Ran had received them kindly beneath the sea.

The giants of the sea

References to feasting and to the great cauldrons of Aegir may also be linked with Celtic myths of the cauldrons of plenty from the land beneath the waves. Aegir has connections with the giants,

and Snorri identifies him with Hymir, the giant who went fishing with Thor. Aegir's nine daughters are said to be the mothers of Heimdall. There are stories also of giantesses from under the sea who could stop ships on their course by seizing them by the prow. Such a woman of the sea was Wachilt, who is mentioned in a late saga and was said to be the mother of the giant Wade. She stayed for a while on land with a king, and then went back to the sea, and stopped the ship of the king by seizing it as he was on a journey, to announce that she was to bear him a son. It is presumably the same giantess who came to the help of a descendant of Wade, carrying both him and his horse beneath the waves when he was pursued by his enemies.

Stone of the eleventh century from Ramsundberg, Södermanland, in Sweden, which represents the story of the slaying of the dragon by Sigurd the Volsung. The dragon forms the border of the picture, and is stabbed by the hero, and inside Sigurd can be seen roasting the heart on a skewer, and sucking his burnt thumb. The talking birds perch on the tree to which Sigurd's horse Grani is tied, and the smith, beheaded by Sigurd, can be seen with his tools to the right.

Memories of Wade survived in both Scandinavian and Anglo-Saxon tradition, and he was said to be the father of the more famous Weland. He was consistently associated with water, and was once said to have waded over the sea that separates two of the Danish islands with his little son in his arms. The underworld extended beneath the sea as well as the earth, and both land and sea giants had connections with the Vanir. In the myths the sea is recognised as a power of destruction, as indeed it must have proved to many families, and beneath the waves lay the serpent who was ultimately to overwhelm the earth. Yet its water was also the source of inspiration and life. When the land was covered by the sea at Ragnarok, it was to rise again, purified, for a further cycle of existence.

Hoenir and Ull

Not much is known about the other gods. Hoenir, the silent god, may have been an ancient deity of some importance, since he was one of

Another carving showing the roasting of the dragon's heart, on a stone of about A.D. 1000 from Andreas in the Isle of Man. Sigurd roasts the heart, cut on slices, over the flames, and has his burnt thumb in his mouth, while his horse looks on.

the three who created man. He was said to be swift and long-legged, and on account of this attempts have been made to identify him with various birds, including the raven of Odin. The name of Ull was long remembered, since many places called after him are found in Sweden and south Norway, though not in Denmark. He was said to be a warrior, skilled on skis and with the bow, and the shield was called his ship. Skadi also went about on snowshoes and carried a bow, and there may have been some confusion between these two figures. Saxo has a tale of how Odin was expelled from his kingship over the gods because of his behaviour in forcing Rind to bear a son, and how Ull, whom Saxo calls Ollerus, took his place. He describes Ull as a magician who crossed the sea on a magic bone, which might suggest ice skates. If he is a god connected with winter, however, it is strange to find that his name seems to be related to a Gothic word meaning 'glory' or 'brightness', and he may be an early sky god. It is possible that he was another of the many deities associated with the Vanir.

The god Forseti

Another god briefly mentioned by Snorri is Forseti, the son of Balder. He dwelt in a hall of gold and silver called Glitnir and was a bringer of peace. In an eighth-century Life of St. Willebrod, there is a story of the saint visiting an island between Frisia and Denmark, where there was a sacred spring. Willebrod baptized three men in the spring, and killed a cow in the holy place, which resulted in his being taken prisoner and condemned to death. But when lots were taken to decide which man should be sacrificed, Willebrod escaped three times, and so the king spared his life. The island was called Fositesland, and another place named after the god was near Oslo Fiord. Another story from a Frisian source tells how twelve Frisians were summoned by Charles the Great to give an account of their laws, but could not do so. They were condemned to death, but chose the alternative of being set adrift in a rudderless boat, calling on God to help them. As they were going aboard, a thirteenth man joined their company, with a golden axe on his shoulder. He steered the ship with his axe, and when they reached land he threw it into the ground, causing a spring to gush up, and then taught them the laws they needed to know before he left them. Although this professes to be a Christian legend, it might be a memory of an almost forgotten local deity, associated with the axe, the teaching of law, and gold and silver, perhaps the ancient sky god under a different name.

The minor deities

These are the main deities mentioned in the myths, although other names occur from time to time, and titles and epithets abound in the poems and in Snorri's account, causing some confusion. Sometimes titles may have been personified in the literature as independent figures, as seems to have been the case with Bragi, called the god of poetry. There is a tiny figure Byggvir, 'barley', who is said to chatter in Freyr's ear. His wife, Beyla, may take her name from the bee whose honey was used in brewing mead. The Beow or Beaw named among the ancestors of Anglo-Saxon kings was at one time taken to be a deity connected with barley, but the names before Woden have now

been shown to be a late and artificial addition to the list. The sons of Thor, Modi and Magni, suggest personifications of his mighty strength. Vidar, like Hoenir, is called the silent god. It is he who slays the wolf after Odin has been devoured, and he and Vali, the son born to Rind to avenge Balder, are said with the children of Thor to survive into the new age. Such minor figures provide interesting problems for scholars, who can speculate endlessly concerning their origins, but they are unlikely to have been deities who received worship from men, or about whom important myths were created. They have their place in the additional lore attached to the main cults. The poems illustrate how copious and complex was the teaching about the gods and their world, and what a rich vocabulary attached to the mythology of the Viking Age. Snorri works hard to produce a consistent whole from such names and titles as he finds in the poems, but he often shows that he himself is baffled.

Man surrounded by snakes portrayed on the back of the little wooden wagon found in the Oseberg ship, thought to be used for ceremonial purposes. This figure has no harp, and therefore need not be identified with the hero Gunnar, who is pictured on other carvings playing a harp in a snakepit while his hands are bound.

The world of the gods

The account of the gods and goddesses who make up Asgard and people the underworld is a confusing one, but the mythological picture of the world in which the gods, the giants and mankind are set is reasonably clear. Information about it occupies a considerable part of the mythological poems, and was clearly thought to be of some importance in the last period of heathenism. We are told of its creation, of its division into separate regions, and of its final destruction, when one age comes to an end and a new race of men and divine beings arises to repeople the world in the age to come.

The World Tree

The walled city of Asgard where the gods dwelt was part of a much larger world picture. The centre of the whole was the World Tree, Yggdrasil, which the poems describe at length. This was the guardian tree of the gods, with roots stretching into three realms, the kingdoms of the gods, the giants and the dead. In all it was said to link together nine worlds. It is implied that the seat of Odin, from which he could look into all the worlds at once, was set in this tree. Sometimes it seems as if he might be identified with the eagle on the crest of Yggdrasil, with a hawk perched on its forehead. This eagle had a twin, a giant eagle said to crouch at the northern end of the sky, whose name means Swallower of Corpses. He may originally have been linked with the giant in eagle form who is hostile to the gods. This giant appears in a number of myths, for instance in the story of the stealing of the apples of youth. This may be yet another instance of the symbolism dimly discerned in the literature, that of the high god Odin opposed and shadowed by a giant ruler of the kingdom of death. The form of this opposition has, however, become very confused, since sometimes the rival power appears to be Loki, or Utgard-Loki, and sometimes Loki himself battles against it.

At the foot of the tree lay a huge serpent, who is presumably the same as the World Serpent, coiled round the inhabited earth and hidden in the depths of the sea. The serpent is at war with the eagle, and a nimble squirrel is said to run up and down the tree, carrying insulting messages from one to the other.

The idea of a tree which marks the centre of the world, with an eagle at the top and a serpent at the foot, is a symbol found far beyond Scandinavia. It is of great antiquity, and may be recognised in art of a very early period. It

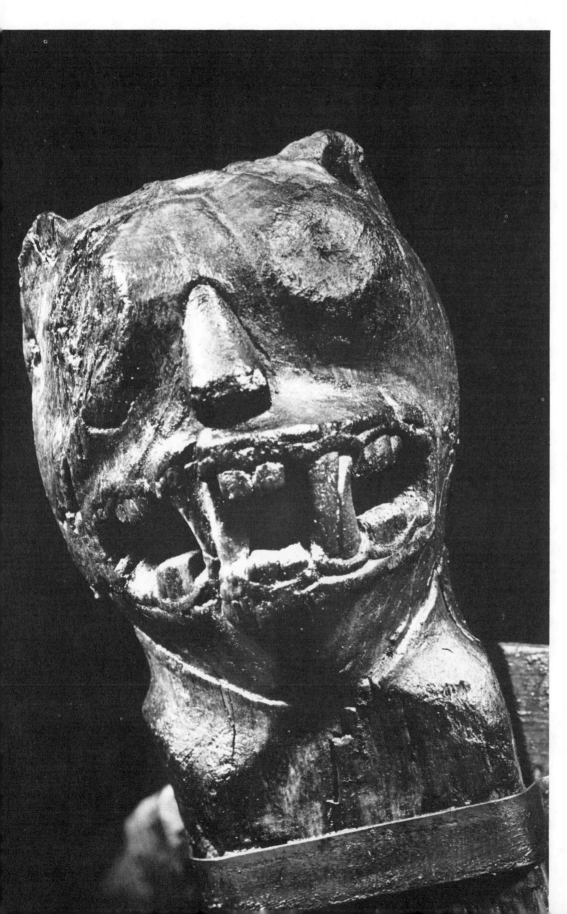

A carved head from 'Shetelig's sledge', one of the four sledges found in the Oseberg ship, and probably used at the funeral. The heads on these are all menacing and grim, as if representing malevolent monsters of the underworld.

seems to have been a dominating symbol in the religious thought of a large part of Europe and Asia long before the Viking Age, and much concerning it may still be found in the myths and legends of the Finno-Ugrian people and in the lore of shamanism. Familiar too is the conception expressed in the Edda poems, that the tree is continually being destroyed and yet continually renewed. In this sense it is eternal, and the implication is that while the worlds perish and the gods are slain, the tree continues through the ages, and shelters and gives birth to new life. The destruction of the tree comes from serpents which gnaw at its roots, and harts and goats which feed on the branches. It is from the milk of a goat which devours the leaves of the tree that the bright mead drunk in the hall of Odin is said to be derived, while from the horns of the great hart in the sky come fast-flowing rivers. Honey-dew falls from the tree down on to the earth. This is the same symbolism as that of the life-giving tree which produces nourishment for gods and men, found in the Near East.

Figurehead of a ship in the form of a monster with long neck and biting teeth, from a Viking Age ship. It was recovered from the River Scheldt. British Museum.

The spring beneath the tree

At the tree's foot is a spring, perhaps more than one, whose water possesses power. There is the spring of Mimir, said to be in the kingdom of the gods, beneath one of the roots, from which Odin drank in his quest for wisdom, sacrificing one of his eyes as a payment for the water. There is also a spring tended by the three Norns deciding the destinies of men. Beside this spring the gods were said to hold their assembly, riding daily over the bridge Bifrost which men call the rainbow, the bridge built by the gods to join earth and heaven. There were two swans in this spring, which sounds like an echo of the symbolism of the Bronze Age. From it the Norns are said to water the tree Yggdrasil. There is clearly a link between the tree and man's fate, because it seems to be viewed, as in some shamanistic teaching, as the source of unborn souls.

Odin on the World Tree

Yggdrasil is called an ash in the poems, although sometimes it seems to be the sacred evergreen, the yew. It has links also with the other sacred tree of the Germanic peoples, the oak, which was associated with the cult of the god of the sky and was often said to have a spring at its foot. The name Yggdrasil appears to be linked with Odin, one of whose many names was *Yggr*, and the most satisfactory interpretation seems to be 'Horse of Ygg.' If this is the correct one, then it must be based on the belief that Odin himself hung on the tree, and 'rode' on it as men were said to 'ride' on the gallows-tree. In one of the poems Odin claimed to have hung on the World Tree for nine days and nights, pierced with a spear as a sacrifice to himself, in the manner in which his victims were wont to hang. After the nine nights of fasting and agony, he was able to obtain knowledge of the magical runes for men, the symbols of knowledge and mantic wisdom. This idea of the god dying on the tree can hardly be based on the Christian crucifixion, since it is fully in accordance with many accounts of the initiation of the shaman in different regions. He has to suffer the pangs of torture and death, often linked with the symbolism of the World Tree, and he has to come back to life again before he can possess the gifts needed to practise shamanism.

The tree at the centre

The function of the tree at the centre of the earth was to join earth and heaven, for the eagle on the branches was the bird of the sky and the serpent the creature of the underworld. Midgard, or Middle Earth, the abode of Mankind, was created around the tree, while the tree's roots stretched down into the other worlds, the spirit worlds into which men might sometimes penetrate. According to this picture, the world of the gods is reached by a descent into the earth, although at the same time it is sometimes represented as a series of levels in the tree itself, and the nine worlds of the poems are said to be 'in the tree.' Finno-Ugrian mythology, as well as Christian apocalyptic literature, has a tradition of a series of heavens, one above the other. It would be far from simple to trace the various influences which have created this apparently contradictory picture. In any case, since this is an image of realms outside time and space, we must not expect consistent geographical details. This is the lore of the Other World, a map of the adventures of the spirit, and vivid and powerful as the imagery is, it will not be expressed in rational terms of distance and direction.

The road to the other world

Although the tree forms a link between the worlds of gods and men and the realm of the dead, there is another set of symbols which emphasise the huge and terrifying spaces which separate these kingdoms. Only a god in bird form or a supernatural horse like Sleipnir can pass swiftly from one to another. The poems describe a long and perilous journey over mountains and through forests, across dangerous rivers and through mist and darkness, and finally over a high gate shutting off the Other World from men. This gate is presented under various names as the barrier dividing the dead from the living, and Sleipnir leapt over this when he took Odin down into Hel. There is also at least one bridge, called the Echoing Bridge, over which Balder and other dead are said to ride while it reverberates beneath their feet, but which gives out a different sound when a living man passes over it. A maiden or giantess guards this bridge, and challenges those who pass over, as Brynhild was challenged in one of the Edda poems when she

Carving from the stave church at Urnes, Norway, which recalls the symbolism of the World Tree as described in the literature, ceaselessly devoured by hart and serpent.

passed through to the land of the dead to claim Sigurd for her husband.

The creation

We are told enough concerning the creation of the worlds of gods and men to make it clear that this formed an important part of pre-Christian teaching, as in most mythologies. The earth was formed from chaos, out of a great emptiness known as Ginnungagap. The concept behind this name seems to be that of inner reality behind an outward appearance which conceals it, like the deceiving magic which Utgard-Loki practised on Thor, and which is called *sjonhverfing*, deceiving of the eyes, when used by witches in the sagas. Behind the apparent emptiness of chaos in the abyss existed potential life. How this was revealed is told in various ways. One explanation is that the fiery realm of Muspell in the south came into contact with the cold frozen wastes of the north, and as the fire met the ice, it melted it, and from the melting ice the giant Ymir took shape. He was the ancestor of all

giants, and he was nourished by another primeval creature, a cow which licked the salty ice-blocks until they formed another being called Buri.

One tradition is that the first man and woman grew out of the left armpit of the giant Ymir, while from his two feet the race of frost giants was engendered. But the giant was slain by three gods, the sons of Bor who was the son of Buri, and these three set to work to form the world from Ymir's body. They used his flesh for the soil, his bones for mountains and stones, his hair for vegetation and his blood for the sea. From the dome of his skull they formed the sky, giving it to four dwarfs to raise high above the earth, while his brains formed the clouds. The race of dwarfs bred like maggots in the body of Ymir, and came out of the hills and rocks when the world was created. The name of the primeval giant has been related to the Sanskrit *yama* and interpreted as 'hybrid' or 'hermaphrodite', the single being who gave birth to male and female beings. This is confirmed by the name given by Tacitus to the first ancestor of the Germanic people, whom he calls Tuisto, the father of Mannus. This name is thought to mean a two-fold being. Ymir might be regarded not only as the source of both man and woman, but also of both men and giants, so that man shares his ancestry with the beings of the Other World.

The primeval giant, who is slain to create the world, and the primeval cow can be found in other mythologies. There is no trace, however, of the other widespread creation myth, known to the Finns, of the origin of the world in a primeval egg. As for the three gods who slew the giant, these are known to Snorri as Odin, Vili and Ve. Not much more is heard concerning these brothers of Odin, but there are references to them in early skaldic verse, and according to one tradition they took over his kingdom and his wife during his absence. The same three gods, according to Snorri, created man and woman from two trees on the seashore, calling them Ask and Embla. The first god gave them life, the second understanding, and the third the senses and outward appearance, if this is the correct interpretation of some rather obscure terms used in one of the poems. The poem *Völuspá* however makes the three gods who created man Odin, Hoenir and Loki.

The world of men was said to be protected from the giants by a wall made from the eyebrows of Ymir. The world of the gods was also

A man pursued by a monster on one of the Gotland stones, from Austers Hangvar, of about A.D. 500. National Historical Museum, Stockholm.

guarded by a wall, built by the giant who was never paid for his work, the owner of the wonderful horse which sired Sleipnir. The gods caused time to exist for men, sending Night and Day driving in swift chariots round the heavens, or, as an alternative image, two fair children, Sun and Moon, journeying across the sky. This appears to be a late echo of the double journey of the chariot in the Bronze Age. Sun is a maiden who drives furiously, because she knows that a wolf pursues her and longs to devour her, while another wolf would swallow up the Moon if he could.

The elves and fair giants

There are other inhabitants of the universe besides gods, men and giants. Elves are mentioned, both light elves and dark, and Alfheim, their home, is sometimes represented as one of the nine worlds. Because they had passed into folklore and become a small, homely people by the time the stories were written down, it is hard to tell whether the fair elves were once the same as the fair giants, who are distinct from the evil frost giants and may perhaps be associated with the Vanir. The dark elves might then be identified with their enemies, the hostile giants, who wished to destroy the Sun and Moon and the dwellings of the gods and re-establish chaos and death.

The realm of Gudmund

Some of the most puzzling and interesting stories which survive in the legendary sagas relate to King Gudmund of Glasisvellir, the 'Glittering Plains', who is said to reside in the Land of the Not-Dead. He is visited by various heroes, who pass through thick forests and mist and darkness and sometimes make a sea voyage to reach his abode, and he has twelve beautiful daughters, who are described as fair women of giant stature, riding on red horses. Sometimes the hero is befriended by one of these daughters, who takes him as her lover. She may resent his return to a Christian environment. For example, one of the men of Olaf Tryggvason was blinded by one of the giant maidens on his departure from Gudmund's realm back to the court of the Christian king. Gudmund is a neighbour of the sinister Geirrod and his brood, the giants visited and ultimately slain by Thor, and there is hostility between them. There are certain resemblances between Gudmund's realm and the fairy world visited by mortals in Celtic literature, but

Part of the east face of the Gosforth Cross from Cumberland, showing a warrior with a spear, and below a man greeted by a woman with a horn closely resembling those on the Gotland stones who are thought to represent valkyries welcoming the dead to the realm of Odin.

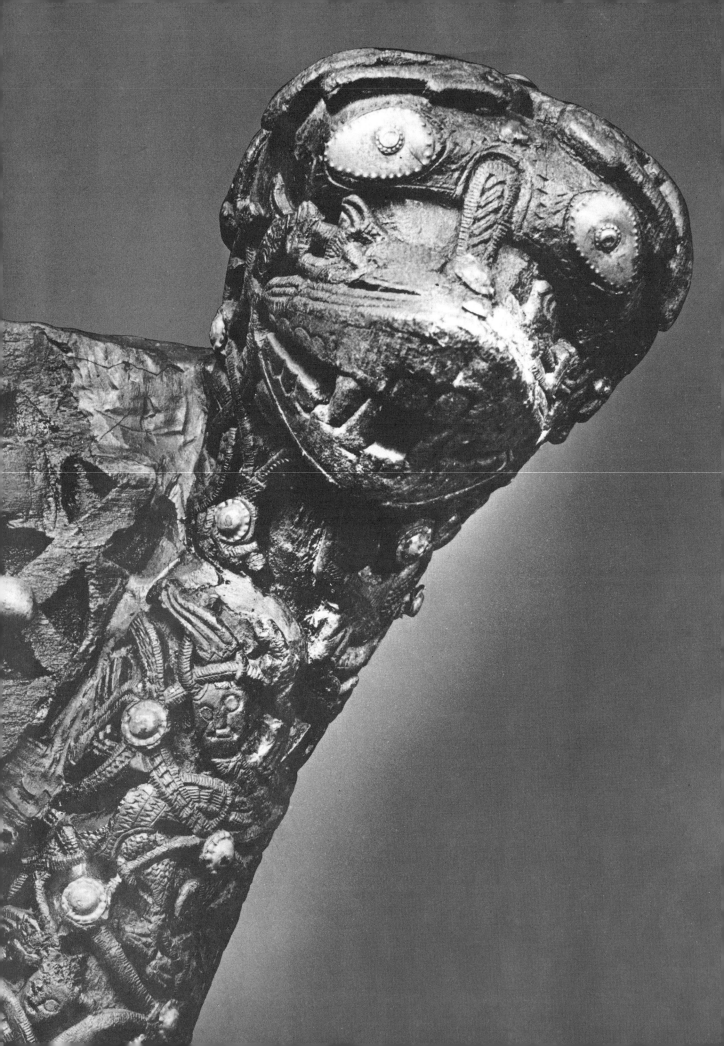

on the other hand there is a firm tradition that his kingdom may be reached by travelling eastwards beyond Sweden. It lies apparently on the other side of the Baltic.

Elves and land-spirits

There seems to be some link between the elves and the dead within the earth, who still benefit men and who may be born again into the world through their descendants. The early king Olaf, thought to be reborn in the person of the Christian king Olaf the Holy, was called 'Elf of Geirstad', and sacrifices were said to be made

Iceland, a new and uninhabited country, to come to terms with them and win their favour. There are references in the sagas to mountain or cliff-giants, who were linked with certain features of the Icelandic landscape. One such supernatural figure was called Bard, and was said to dwell in a cave on Snaefell, to have a bevy of fair daughters, like Gudmund, and to be visited by young men whom he instructed in ancient lore. He was called the god of Snaefell. There may have originally been a link between such figures and one of the main cults, but it had become obscure by the time such stories were recorded.

to him and also to elves dwelling in mounds. Another race of beings linked closely with the earth were the land-spirits, said to follow 'lucky' men and to give help with hunting and fishing. They were believed to dwell in hills, stones and rivers, and they sometimes appeared in animal form or as little men and women. It was said to be forbidden to bring ships into harbour with menacing figureheads, because they might frighten the land-spirits. It seems to have been on such powers that the seeresses called for help when they sought to discover hidden things, since they might help or hinder them on their mantic journeys.

Giants in the mountains

Such spirits do not seem to be regarded as ancestral, linked with particular families, but rather as powers who resided in the very land itself. It was of the utmost importance for settlers in

Possibly such traditions were part of the early esoteric practices associated with the Vanir.

In Norway Dovrefell was similarly regarded as the home of a giant Dofri, who was said to have been helped by Harald Fairhair in his boyhood, and who in return helped and supported the king all his life, and was visited by him from time to time. Dofri is said to have trained Harald in ancient lore, to have taught him various skills, and to have urged him to work for the sovereignty of Norway, giving him aid in his struggle. There are conflicting stories about Harald's connection with this giant, and about the giant's daughter whom in some versions he is said to have married. In one tale Harald preserved the body of his dead wife, until a wise man delivered the king from the baleful influence which she had cast over him. In another his 'fostermother' on Dovrefell is represented as a hideous troll woman, to whom the king sent a present of a

Centre and above: two views of the fourth sledge from the Oseberg burial, showing creatures with birdlike or feline faces and staring eyes. All the sledges are probably ninth century work and can be seen in the Ship Museum near Oslo.

Far left: a carved head from 'Gustafson's sledge', recovered from the Oseberg ship.

keg of butter and two flitches of bacon. Behind these confused stories there are hints at some pre-Christian cult, which has obvious links with that of the Vanir, but which sometimes suggests the cult of Odin. Tales of Dovrefell lingered on in folklore long after the heathen period.

The homes of the gods

The traditions of entry into caves and mountains to meet supernatural beings are in agreement with the representation of the world of the gods existing below the earth or under the water. The rainbow bridge joining earth and heaven emphasises the link with both earth and sky. The lines dividing the supernatural beings were no doubt never very clearly drawn, and when heathenism became a matter of ancient lore passed down into Christian times, the distinctions grew more blurred and confused. The gods had continual dealings with the giants, by no means always hostile, and visited their abodes. In many cases they married their daughters.

The shrines and holy places of the deities were closely linked with the earth and with local features of the landscape, particularly when the sanctity of a holy spot had been established for centuries and it had become a centre for offerings, either to the gods of battle or to the powers of fertility. The tombs of dead kings might also be centres of religious rites and traditions, so that these to some extent represented the dwelling places of the gods in the world of mankind, while the tradition of a supreme sky god continued at the same time. The break with this tradition of the sacred earth and water of the homeland, once men left Norway and Sweden to settle in Iceland, must have been abrupt and far-reaching, although some of the early settlers found places in the new land to reverence. At Holyfell, for example, the dead of certain families were said to congregate after death. It was the sky god Thor above all who left an impression on the imagination of the Icelandic storytellers who look back on the heathen period, and this is hardly surprising.

Dwarfs and monsters

The picture of the universe which takes shape from the myths is that of the round earth of men with the sea surrounding it, and the World Tree marking its centre. The dwarfs who supported the sky over the heads of men may be seen on some of the hogback memorial stones of the Viking period which survive in northern

England. On many sculptured stones also are found the monsters of the darkness, the serpent and the dragon. The image of the devouring monster is first seen in Scandinavian art of the Migration period, and there is a vivid representation of him about to swallow a little human figure on one of the memorial stones of this period in Gotland. Whereas serpents in earlier periods seem to be associated with healing and the blessing of the dead rather than with horror, the idea of the serpent or dragon as an image of engulfing death may have become a dominant one at about the time when the cult of Odin became important in the North. The idea of twisted, venomous serpents writhing in interlacing coils and surrounding the hero in a snakepit is found in both literary tradition and in art. This may have been partly derived from Christian literary traditions, but seems to have its roots in vigorous heathen tradition also.

The fiery dragon

In Anglo-Saxon England it was the fiery dragon, breathing out flame and passing over the habitations of men like a dangerous comet shedding fire, which was the dominant image. The dragon was said to dwell in the gravemound, and there to guard the rich treasures buried with the dead, while remaining, as one Anglo-Saxon poet put it, no whit the better for it. In the second part of the heroic poem *Beowulf*, such a dragon from a burial mound, infuriated because a man had robbed his treasure-hoard of a rich cup, attacked the people of the Geats by dropping fire on their houses, so that their king Beowulf had to go out against the monster in his old age to deliver his people from the nightly terror. Beowulf went down before the flames from the dragon's jaws and its sharp teeth, although he and one faithful thane, remaining when all the rest fled, slew the dragon after a terrible struggle.

There are also accounts of Scandinavian dragon fights. Sigurd the Volsung overcame Fafnir through cunning, stabbing him from beneath as he crawled over the earth. The hero Ragnar Lodbrok strengthened his clothes with pitch so that they would resist the flames of the dragon, and succeeded in overcoming him. Scandinavian dragons also guarded hoards of treasure, and it is implied in some of the tales that a dead man in his mound could be transformed, like Fafnir, into a dragon lying upon the gold. But in the Scandinavian stories it is on the serpent aspect of the dragon that most stress is laid. It might

be the influence of the Roman dragon banner, the windsleeve carried by Roman legions based on the image of the flying dragon of the East, which inspired the vivid symbolism of the flying monster of the Anglo-Saxon poems. It has recently been shown that the picture of the Geats in *Beowulf* may have been based largely on confused literary traditions about the Scythians and the Getae, including the gold-guarding griffins of the Black Sea region. On the other hand, the creature that appears on the shield of Sutton Hoo might be an illustration of Beowulf's dragon, with its pairs of folded wings and jaws filled with terrible biting teeth. Shooting stars and comets were said in the Chronicle of the Anglo-Saxons to be fiery dragons flying through the air, signs of ill-omen. It seems possible then that many separate influences are involved in the concept of this mythological crea-

Above: roof of the twelfth-century stave church at Borgund, Norway, showing the carved wooden figures of dragons on the gables.

Left: a dragon head with gaping jaws from the roof of the stave church at Lom, Norway.

ture, and the link between dragon and grave-mound might be explained not only by the idea of a guardian of treasure in the earth, but also by the imagery of the funeral pyre and the fierce flames devouring the dead, so vividly described in *Beowulf*. There is ample archaeological evidence from pre-Christian times in Anglo-Saxon England that burning of the dead on an impressive scale was well-established in many districts before the conversion, and that it continued as late as the seventh century.

The destruction of the world

The created world was doomed to destruction, and we are reminded of this not only in the famous poem *Völuspá*, the poem from which Snorri derived much of his impressive account of Ragnarok, but also by many references to the destruction of the world elsewhere in Germanic and Scandinavian literature. There may well have been some influence here from Christian traditions of the end of the world and the last judgement, but this can hardly account for the picture as a whole, especially in view of parallel myths and traditions outside Scandinavia from non-Christian mythologies. *Völuspá* itself may have been inspired partly by the experience, either first-hand or from vivid accounts from those who had witnessed it, of a major volcanic eruption in Iceland, such as we know took place at relatively frequent intervals in historic times. The picture of intense cold as a background for mounting fire and smoke rising to the stars, in conjunction with a tidal wave which engulfed the inhabited land, may have drawn much of its vigour and terror from some such remembered catastrophe. The account, however, links up with traditions found elsewhere in the literature, and particularly with that of the final battle between the gods and the monsters, which is portrayed on a number of memorial stones of the Viking Age.

It is evident in the poems that the death of Balder was much more than a personal loss and defeat for Odin. In some way it ushered in the doom of the gods. There were evil omens before Balder fell, and the gods dreamed evil dreams. In the world of men there was much warfare and deeds of hatred and treachery, while the bonds of loyalty to leader and kindred, so powerful in the early Viking Age, seemed to be breaking. There was also a period of bitter and unrelieved cold, the mighty winter, when for three years no summer came to relieve men of their

Far left: cross in the churchyard at Gosforth, Cumberland, of about A.D. 1000, a splendid piece of sculpture which unfortunately is deteriorating fast through exposure to weather. It shows the crucifixion of Christ and also a number of figures representing the battles between gods and monsters at Ragnarok. At the top a man confronts a serpent with gaping jaws, while the woman below the formalised crucifixion scene resembles those carrying horns on the Gotland stones. A dragon figure can be seen below.

Left: part of the west face, showing a woman with a bowl beside a bound man. They are believed to represent the captive Loki with his wife Signy who protected him from the poison of the serpents.

sufferings. The implication is that now at last the sun had been caught by the wolf which had long pursued her, and that this was Fenriswolf, breaking from the bonds that Tyr had laid on him. Certainly he was said to break free and to advance with huge jaws opened wide between earth and heaven, while at the same time the World Serpent emerged from the waves, blowing out poison over the world, and bringing with him a flood to overwhelm the earth. As the sea advanced on the land, a ship came with it, carrying a crew of giants with Loki steering it. The ship is said to have been built of the uncut nails of dead men, apparently a folk tradition. From the fiery realm of Muspell, which in the beginning had caused the creation of life, destruction now came, for Surt at the head of the sons of Muspell rode across the slender rainbow bridge Bifrost, and it broke under the weight of the terrible host.

Now the gods had been roused to their danger by the horn of Heimdall, and Odin went to take counsel with the head of Mimir and knew that

Centre: hogback tombstone from Heysham, Lancashire, of the Viking Age. Four figures support the sky, like the dwarfs described in the *Prose Edda*, and it is possible that this scene may represent the creation.

Below: one of two hogback tombstones in Gosforth Church, Cumberland, found under the church during restoration and now built into the floor. It shows two armies advancing, perhaps representing the last battle at Ragnarok, and resembles scenes on the Gotland stones. The stones are much worn, but have been carved by a sculptor of great ability.

the time had come to fight. He led out his champions to a great plain, where the last battle must take place. He himself however did not fall before hostile weapons, but was swallowed by his ancient enemy, the wolf. His young son Vidar took vengeance for his father's death, seizing the wolf and rending its jaws asunder. On its lower jaw he set his foot, clad according to Snorri in a special shoe which had been in the making since time began. It was made of the snips of leather which shoemakers must throw away when they shape heel and toe, so as to help the Aesir in their last struggle. But though Odin was avenged, it was too late to save Asgard. Thor went out to meet the serpent, and slew it, but the poison from its mouth overcame him, and he fell dead beside it in his hour of victory. Tyr fought with the hound Garm that guarded Hel, Heimdall did battle with Loki, and all were slain. Freyr went out against Surt, but fell fighting. Surt alone was left alive to fling fire over earth and heaven, so that the flames mounted as the earth sank beneath the waves.

The renewal of life

Only the World Tree did not fall, although it shook and trembled as worlds were shattered around it. Within this tree were sheltered two beings, called Lif and Lifthrasir, who were the man and woman destined to repeople the earth when it rose again from the sea. Perhaps it was in the tree also that the gods' sons were sheltered, since they were said to survive the conflict and to join Balder returned from the dead. The earth rose again from the water, cleansed of all the terror and destruction, green and fair as at the beginning of time. A new sun, more radiant than her mother, encircled the heavens, and the eagle, symbol of the god of the sky, was seen on the mountains. This renewal and opening of another cycle after the universal cataclysm is found also in mythologies of the East. The story

of a great winter from which certain privileged beings were sheltered occurs in an early Persian myth. The possibility of influences from the East coming through Russia into Sweden, to help to create this great and impressive picture of the world's end in the Viking Age, is one to be borne in mind, although there are isolated references to a belief in the destruction of the world in earlier pre-Christian sources.

Carvings of the last battle

There is some evidence also that such ideas were not limited to scholars and to scholarly written traditions after the close of the heathen period. Scenes on the tenth-century Gosforth cross in Cumberland seem to be based on knowledge of battles between gods and monsters, although this is a Christian monument. There is, first, a figure which is thought to be the bound Loki with his wife bending over him. There is a male figure encountering a monster and holding open its jaws with hand and foot, as Vidar is said to have done when meeting the wolf. There is also a figure with a horn, and a mounted warrior. Such considerable agreement with the literary account of the last battle indicates that the scenes have been deliberately set in a Christian context, in conjunction with the crucifixion of Christ, to illustrate the struggle against the forces of evil. On two worn but impressive hogback stones now built into the floor of the church at Gosforth there are figures struggling against serpents and two armies approaching each other, as if for the last great battle. A tenth-century slab from Kirk Andreas in the Isle of Man shows a man with an eagle on his shoulder and with the characteristic *valknut* beside him. His leg is between the jaws of a wolf, and almost certainly the figure represents the devouring of Odin. Scenes on other carved stones have been interpreted, with less plausibility, as symbols of the last battle.

The fall of Odin

There is little doubt that it is on Odin and the defeat of his champions that the main emphasis is laid, the fight with the wolf, the battle between the hosts, and the binding of Loki being all linked with this. The fates of the other gods in *Völuspá* appear to be an extension of this tradition, further developed by Snorri from hints found in other myths. For example, Thor's battle with the serpent and Heimdall's fight with Loki are brought into the Ragnarok scene, and Freyr, who gave his sword away for the wooing of Gerd, is said to be weaponless when he meets Surt. The significance of the story of the last battle, however, is also the ending of the old order, when the gods go down fighting against odds too great for them. The civilisation precariously set up by man is destroyed by the forces he has long kept in check, and overwhelmed by water and fire, which once nourished and preserved him. This is a characteristic comment on the vulnerability and mutability of human achievement.

A Norwegian mill at Eidsvag on Moldefjord, the kind of background from which the Viking ships sailed out on their voyages of trade and adventure.

Far left: a view of Thingvellir in Iceland, seen from the place where the All-Thing or General Assembly of Icelandic chieftains met once a year, for the making of laws and settlements of disputes. The Assembly opened on Thursday, the day sacred to Thor, and the chieftains, many of whom acted as priests for their districts, paid honour to him and to other gods as the powers who had established law and order among men. It was here that the decision to adopt Christianity was taken in the year A.D. 1000.

Left: gold bracteate from Riseley, Kent, which shows a man between two serpent-like monsters. It may be compared with the similar group on the Sutton Hoo purse and with other examples from Scandinavia. Institute of Archaeology, Oxford.

Below: an amulet in silver in the form of a hammer on a chain, from Odeshög, Ostergotland, Sweden, of tenth century date. The staring eyes and stylised beard combine with the hammer shape to symbolise the powers of Thor as god of the sky, while the type of hammer suggests a weapon hurled through the air rather than a smith's tool. National Historical Museum, Stockholm.

The coming of Christianity

It is always necessary to remind ourselves that the myths as we have them have been recorded in a Christian age and written down in Christian monasteries. They must therefore have been coloured to some extent by the thought of men who had repudiated the old faith, although how much this has been the case has remained a subject of lively discussion ever since interest in Scandinavian mythology quickened with the production of dictionaries and the editing of texts in the last century.

There are many parallels between the myths and the teaching of the Christian church. The idea of a dying god who rose again was already present in the fertility cults, and even the divine figure hanging upon a tree formed part of the myths concerning Odin and his acquisition of wisdom. The little child coming from a divine world to rule men seems also to have been familiar in the teachings about the Vanir. The bound demon in the earth and the conception of a coming doomsday with all its attendant horrors appear to have formed part of heathen tradition before they came in with the teaching of the church. The idea of Christ as a brave young warrior at the head of a group of faithful thanes is developed in the early Christian poetry of Anglo-Saxon England, showing how the new faith could be presented in a form acceptable to men reared on the heathen traditions of a heroic past. The courageous band of early missionaries and martyrs upheld this heroic conception of the new faith. Suggestions have been made that all such resemblances between the earlier myths and the new religion are due to deliberate imitation by Christians who recorded the myths. But we have archaeological evidence and objective accounts from pre-Christian writers of earlier periods, showing that a foundation for such ideas can be found far back in the pagan past. We also have the testimony of other mythologies from outside both Scandinavia and the Christian world, indicating that these ideas form part of a familiar pattern of development in religious history and symbolism. Moreover, the vigour and power of the myths are not such as one would expect to find in a parody of an alien religion or in an imitation of scholarly writings.

The two cultures

On the other hand, there was certainly a willingness to reconcile pagan teachings with the new faith, the course advocated by the wise Pope Gregory to the first Christian bishops in Anglo-

Stave church of the twelfth century at Fagusnes, Borgund, in Norway.

Right: stave church of the
twelfth century, with a
spire above the wooden
roof, at Gudbrandsdale
in Norway.

Saxon England. One example of this reconciliation is provided by the carved crosses of the Viking Age, of which that at Gosforth is an outstanding example, setting the crucifixion of Christ beside the battles of gods and monsters. A scene from the savage tale of Sigmund, one of Odin's heroes, appears to have been built into Winchester Cathedral when it was enlarged by the Danish king Canute. The Franks Casket, believed to have been made in Northumbria in the seventh century, draws on pre-Christian heroic traditions linked with the cult of Woden, and at the same time on themes from the new classical and Christian learning of the monasteries, including the fostering of Romulus and Remus, the sacking of the temple in Jerusalem,

Small tenth-century
crucifix from a grave in
the cemetery at Birka,
Sweden. The figure of
Christ is elaborately
ornamented in the
northern style, without
any attempt at realism.

and the visit of the Magi to the infant Christ.

This material, both pagan and Christian, has been used with an informed understanding of the implication of the stories and symbols employed and an open-minded acceptance of conflicting traditions remarkable in so early a period. The poem *Völuspá*, composed towards the end of the heathen period in the North, again shows an objective approach and certainly no hostility towards the declining pagan faith, although it appears to anticipate the coming of Christianity in the introduction of the Mighty Ruler who comes to govern the new world.

Even Saxo, who shows his Christian allegiance in every chapter of his history in his priggish impatience with the old gods, nevertheless knew an enormous repertoire of stories about them, and thought it important to record these in detail. The account of Snorri is outstanding in his ability to enter into the poetry and inspiration of the pagan mythology, and in the enlightenment of his introduction in which he seeks to reconcile the stories with Christian beliefs.

Visits from Odin

A number of stories about gods and supernatural beings, folktales rather than myths, are told consciously from a Christian standpoint, and provide interesting evidence as to how men felt about the gods they had once worshipped. Many old stories seem to have been remodelled to link them with the Christian hero-kings such as Olaf Tryggvason and Olaf the Holy. Others deal with the reaction of the old gods to the faith which supplanted them. The Norwegian kings were said to have encountered both Odin and Thor, in tales which express a certain nostalgia for what had been destroyed. On one occasion it was said that an old man with one eye and a hood pulled down over his face came to the hall of Olaf Tryggvason and proved so brilliant a talker that the king sat long into the night listening to stories of past times and ancient kings. At last the bishop persuaded him to go to bed, and when he asked for the stranger next day, none knew what had become of him. It was discovered however that he had been in the kitchen advising the cooks about their work, and that he had given them two sides of beef to cook with the rest. When he learned of this, the king realised that the visitor must have been Odin, or at least the devil in Odin's form, as the story-teller puts it, and had all the meat destroyed.

On another occasion a stranger came to the hall of Olaf the Holy, calling himself Gest and asking to join the king's bodyguard. He wore a cloak, and a broad-brimmed hat hid most of his face. When the king was in bed he sent for Gest and asked whether he could tell him anything entertaining. They talked long of former kings and mighty deeds of the heroes of old, and Gest finally asked King Olaf which of the old kings he most wanted to be like. The king replied that he could not wish to be a heathen man, but if he might keep his Christian faith, then he would probably choose to be King Hrolf

kraki, one of the greatest heroic leaders of the past. Gest then asked if he would not rather be like the king who overcame all enemies and was accomplished in everything, finding poetry coming to him as easily as speech, and possessing the power to give victory in battle. At that the king recognised his visitor as Odin, and in anger he seized a service book to fling it at his head, declaring that he was the last king he would wish to resemble. As he spoke, the stranger vanished.

Meeting with Thor

An encounter between Olaf Tryggvason and Thor is also included in one of the sagas of the king. As he sailed in his splendid ship, the *Long Serpent*, along the coast, Olaf was hailed by a man on the cliff, who asked to be taken on board. Olaf steered towards land, and picked up the man, who was a huge fellow with a red beard, young and handsome. He jested and wrestled with the crew, and they found him a tough opponent, while he told them that they were unworthy followers of the men who had manned the ship when it belonged to the heathen Raud, whom Olaf had put to death. When they found that he knew many stories of the past, they took him to the king, who asked him to show his knowledge. He told Olaf that the land they were now passing had once been inhabited by giants, but all were killed except for two giantesses, who remained to cause terror to the men who came to settle there. So they called on Redbeard to help them, and he said he had come and slain them with his hammer. He had always helped men like this in their need, but now King Olaf was destroying all his friends. Then he grinned maliciously at the king, and dived into the sea.

A more mysterious encounter on the same voyage south was with a tall man rowing a small boat and moving at a great rate. He was at last overtaken by the *Long Serpent*, and the king hailed him and said he wanted to talk with him. The man however refused to meet the king, who had, he said, treated his friends so cruelly. He went on to say that his grey-haired brother was now far away, but had they been together they would never have yielded nor run away. He refused to tell his name, but threw the oars out of the boat, upset it, and disappeared into the water. It is not clear which god he represents, but here possibly we have a last echo of the tradition of two brother gods.

The rejection of the Vanir

No direct meetings of this kind with the Vanir deities are described, but it is interesting to note that they are represented either as wooden images or as trolls. There is a long account of Olaf Tryggvason's visit to one of Freyr's temples in Thrandheim, where the people were still sacrificing to the god. They claimed that Freyr had long helped them by talking to them, telling them future happenings, and bringing them peace and plenty. The king stopped the sacrifice of a stallion to Freyr, and then took the figure of the god under his arm and carried him to the Assembly. He told them that it was the devil in whom they had trusted, and that the wooden figure in the temple had been given powers in order to delude them. He then chopped up the wooden image, and told them that Freyr had really been a great Swedish king, whose image was put in the burial mound with him after

death, while folk continued to make him gifts of gold and silver. Later on men entered his howe, hoping to remove the treasure, but did not dare to take it out, and only removed the two wooden figures placed there. One they kept for their own worship, and the other they sent to Norway, and this was the one which the king found in the temple. The image of Thorgerd, the goddess worshipped by Jarl Hakon of Halogaland, is described as the figure of a woman with a gold ring on her hand, sitting on a chair and richly adorned with a bright robe given her by Hakon. She also had money chests in which offerings were placed. The king took off her robe, tied her to his horse's tail and dragged her out, asking his men if any of them wanted her for a wife. After he had made sure that none of them reverenced her, he broke what was called the ugly image of Thorgerd with his club, as he had destroyed Freyr's image earlier, and the two were burnt together. This hostile

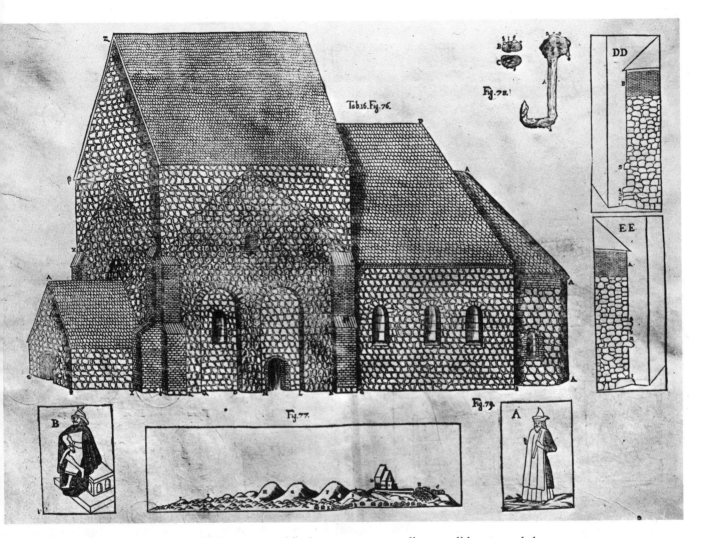

Tab.16.Fig.76.

Fig.78.

DD

EE

Fig.77.

Fig.79.

B

A

picture of Thorgerd, 'wife' to Jarl Hakon and many others, emphasises her link with Freyja, the 'bride' of the Vanir, and with Freyr.

The troll women

Another view of Thorgerd is given in the legendary sagas. The hero Ketill *haengr* is said to have met a troll woman in northern Norway, who told him that she was on her way to a Thing or Assembly of the trolls. This was to be attended by various characters, local deities or landspirits from the surrounding district, and Thorgerd was to be among them. But Ketill had quarrelled with his 'fostermother', the troll whom he encountered in the forest, and she told him that now she had parted company with him.

Another picture of a guardian spirit as a troll is given in the tale of the 'fostermother' of King Harald Fairhair, whose name is given as Heid. She was dressed in a skin kirtle, and had a huge gaping mouth, and she was so tall that the

king's messenger, a tall man, did not reach her shoulder. Harald sent her a ring, just as Jarl Hakon gave a ring to Thorgerd, and with it two flitches of bacon and a barrel of butter, with which she was delighted. She made the two men he sent to her take off their clothes and kiss her, and then she stroked them all over, a familiar method of discovering whether they were to receive wounds, found in saga stories of witchcraft. She foretold what might happen on their journey, and gave them two magic stones, which they could use if attacked by their enemies.

There seems little doubt that in these stories we have an unsympathetic picture of the goddess protectors connected with the Vanir, and sometimes also with Odin. Another slightly less hostile picture is given in one of the legendary sagas, when the hero meets a creature called a *finngálkn*, a word used to describe something which is half human and half animal, like a

Left: a small cross-shaped amulet, half-way between a cross and a Thor's hammer, in silver, found in southern Iceland. It ends in the head of a monster, and must presumably be a heathen symbol.

Above: a drawing from Rudbeck's *Atlantica* of the medieval church at Old Uppsala, Sweden. This church is believed to have been built on the site of an earlier heathen temple. The sketch below shows its position in relation to the royal burial mounds.

centaur. She too had an enormous mouth, and the reason for this is now made clear, for she had the head and tail of a horse, although she is also said to be 'great and impressive.' She offered a splendid sword to the hero, and asked him to kiss her. As he did so, she threw the sword up into the air, so that if he had not leapt forward and embraced her, it would have killed him. The verses spoken by the *finngálkn* have the ring of heroic poetry, and this strange scene appears to be founded on an earlier heathen tradition, the true significance of which is not understood by the storyteller. Such a human figure with an animal head can be seen facing a warrior on the Franks Casket.

The terrors of hell

It is the Vanir and Odin who seem to receive the most hostile treatment in Christian stories about mythological personages. A tale which seems to be aimed directly at Odin and his band of heroes in Valhalla is included as a postscript to one of the sagas of Olaf Tryggvason. One evening the king warned his men that if any of them had to go outside during the night, he must not go alone. The warning, however, was ignored by one man named Thorstein, who could not wake his neighbour and therefore slipped out alone to the privy. The privy was built with eleven seats down either side, and as Thorstein sat next to the door, he saw an evil creature come up through the seat at the furthest end. He asked who he was, and was told that he was one of the heroes who fell fighting with Harald Wartooth of Denmark, come up from Hell. Thorstein asked him who endured the tortures of hell most courageously, and his visitor replied that the bravest there was Sigurd the Volsung, slayer of Fafnir, who was kindling a burning oven. Thorstein at first thought this no very dreadful fate, until the apparition explained that it was Sigurd himself who was used for the kindling. Thorstein then asked who complained the loudest, and the answer was Starkad the Old, who had been one of the most valiant of Odin's heroes. He, the demon said, lay with his ankles in the fire, which at first did not sound very alarming, until it was made clear that only the soles of Starkad's feet protruded from the flames. The demon offered to give Thorstein an illustration of how loudly Starkad yelled in hell. Each time he opened his mouth and shrieked, it was so terrible a sound that Thorstein nearly lost his senses, while the demon moved up three

seats nearer to him with each yell. As he was beginning to utter the third shriek, to show how Starkad yelled at his loudest, Thorstein gave himself up for lost, but at that moment the church bell rang, and the demon sank down into the earth again. The king had missed Thorstein from his bed, realised his danger, and had the bell rung to help him.

Thor after the conversion

Although Thor on the whole emerges rather better than Odin, he is sometimes represented as a coward, losing his strength and courage before the Christian king and his followers. In one tale a young convert called Finn, very hostile towards Thor, beat his image with a club and then tied it to his boat and dragged it through the water. This might have been suggested by the custom of sending the high-seat pillars overboard to that Thor could lead the way to land and show his worshippers where they should settle. Finally Finn cut the image in pieces and put the chips into porridge, which he gave to the dogs to eat, saying that it was right that dogs should eat Thor, since he ate his own sons. This accusation is not explained by the myths which we possess, but might refer

reciting something aloud. Later on a whale came ashore, and they cut it up and ate it, although it made them all ill. Thorhall boasted that he had done this by the poem he had recited to Thor, and that the god had not failed them as Christ had done. When they heard this, they threw the meat away, and before long they were able to catch fish.

The destruction of the shrines

Several stories tell how the king or his converts overthrew the gods from their pedestals and burnt down their shrines. When King Olaf Tryggvason visited Thor's temple in Thrandheim, it was said that Thor was sitting in the midst of the idols in a chariot drawn by two goats. He was adorned with gold and silver, and the model was skilfully made and set on wheels, so that it could move easily along. The king looked at the image, and Skeggi, Thor's worshipper, remarked that he seemed to admire it, and that he was sure that he would have approved of Thor, had he met him. Olaf hastily declared that this was only a likeness of the god, and would have no power against the god of the Christians. Skeggi then asked the king to pull the cord round the horns of the goats, to see how well the chariot moved along, and this Olaf did, after first making the sign of the cross. Skeggi then declared in triumph that he had now become the friend and servant of the god, and had done him reverence. The king in fury lifted his stick and knocked Thor out of the chariot, while his men rushed forward and threw down the idols. In the fight Skeggi was slain.

Thor versus Christ

The sign of the cross made by the king was evidently very similar to that of the hammer made by the worshippers of Thor. The important point is that Skeggi took it as a mark of honour to the god. Similarly when the Christian king Hakon the Good made the sign of the cross over the cup at a sacrificial feast, it was explained to the people that he had made the hammer sign over it in honour of the gods. The little crosses worn by Christians were very similar to the hammer amulets which became popular all over Scandinavia in the tenth century. One mould discovered in Denmark showed that a craftsman might turn out hammers and crosses for heathen men and Christians at the same time.

It was Thor who in the last days of heathenism was regarded as the chief antagonist of Christ.

An artist's conception of the heathen temple at Uppsala, from Rudbeck's *Atlantica*, a manuscript of the late seventeenth century in the Royal Library at Stockholm.

to some story like that of the sacrifice of Thor's goats, who were slain and eaten by the god and then called back to life again by his hammer. Thor's connection with the sea is emphasised again in a tale in one of the Icelandic sagas of a certain Ingjald, who was cursed by a troll woman. He afterwards went out fishing, and was caught in a storm. He saw a red-bearded man in his boat, catching fish with powerful hands, who said that his name was Grim. Ingjald wanted to row back before the storm broke, but Grim said he would have to wait until he had loaded the boat. The wind blew to a gale and darkness came down upon them, while fish-hooks and tackle went overboard. Ingjald wrapped himself in his cloak and gave himself up for lost, and he was only saved by a local guardian spirit, who rowed out to help him. Grim thereupon disappeared into the sea.

There is also a story included in the saga of Erik the Red, telling of Karlsefni's expedition to Vineland, when food ran very short, and a man named Thorhall disappeared. The rest of the company had been praying to God for food, as befitted Christians, but Thorhall decided to appeal to Thor. His companions found him staring at the sky, gaping as if in a trance, and

When Thangbrand, a turbulent Christian who made trouble wherever he went, was sent by Olaf Tryggvason to convert Iceland, since he was something of a liability in Norway, he was said to have been challenged by a number of men in Iceland who supported the old gods. Among his opponents was a woman poet, Steinvor, who was said to hold a public dispute with him, claiming, amongst other things, that Thor

Runic stone raised by King Harald of Denmark in what had been the pagan sanctuary at Jelling, after Harald's conversion to Christianity in the eleventh century. It shows the crucifixion of Christ, but the figure is represented as if in bonds, in accordance with pagan tradition.

had challenged Christ to a duel and Christ had not dared to fight. In a poem which she recited in praise of Thor, she declared that the god had wrecked Thangbrand's ship, while Christ had been unable to protect it.

The driving out of the guardian spirits

There are also stories of how the spirits who had helped men in the past were grievously afflicted by the coming of the new faith, and tormented by the singing of the Christians and

the holy water of the priests. A long story from the Bishops' Sagas tells of a man called Kodran, whose son had been converted to Christianity. Kodran said that he saw what devoted service the Christians gave to their god, and he thought that the bishop who gave them counsel must have second sight. He himself, he said, had always received counsel from a wise man who lived in a great stone near his farm. This man guarded his cattle, gave him good advice, and foretold the future. The bishop was told of this, and he went out with prayers and psalm-singing to the stone and sprinkled holy water on it. He did this each day for three days, and each night the man in the stone came to Kodran in a dream, weeping and lamenting, and urging him to oppose the bishop who was trying to drive him away. He had poured boiling water over his house, he said, so that his little children cried out with the pain. On the second night he appeared in a black cloak of skin, with a gloomy face, in contrast to his splendid array and cheerful appearance in the past. On the third night he declared that he must go out into desolation and exile, and reproached Kodran, whose goods he had always loyally guarded and to whom he had brought prosperity. The change from brightness to gloom and to a dark skin cloak is significant, as here we have the transformation of a heathen deity to a troll taking place before our eyes. Kodran's counsellor took his place among the sad company of trolls and demons who figure in many folktales as enemies of the Christians, although here the sympathy of the storyteller seems to be on the side of the dispossessed spirit.

There is another story of a second-sighted man, Thorhall, who was seen one morning smiling as he lay in his bed beside the window. When asked why, he said that he had seen the hills opening and the creatures who dwelt in them packing their possessions and getting ready to leave. This was said to have taken place before the arrival of Thangbrand the missionary in Iceland. A rather similar story is told of happenings in Norway, when a man had a vision of King Olaf in a dream, telling him that Christianity was about to be preached in his district. He was so impressed by this that he determined to destroy the temple of the old gods. In a neighbouring farm lived a woman with second sight, and early the same day she awoke her men and told them to go out immediately and drive all the animals down from the pastures, and to shut them up in the stables. If they stayed out of doors, she said, not one would be left alive, for her neighbour had become mad and was about to destroy the temple of the gods. They would be driven out in wrath, and would spare no living creature which crossed their path. His men did as she said, and no animal took harm, except for one packhorse which remained outside and was afterwards found dead.

The vengeance of the goddesses

One story has survived about the anticipatory vengeance of the goddesses on the family of Hall of the Side, who was one of the first of the Icelanders to be converted to Christianity. The story is found included in one of the sagas of Olaf Tryggvason. It tells how Hall's eldest son, Thidrandi, a fine young man of eighteen, came home to his father in time to help him to organise the autumn feast, one of the main heathen festivals. There were not many guests, since it was bad weather, and that evening Thorhall, the same man who had seen the spirits departing from the hills because of the approach of the new faith, warned the company not to go outside during the night. After all had gone to bed, Thidrandi, who had given up his bed to a guest and was sleeping in the hall, heard a knocking on the door. This came three times, and at last Thidrandi, thinking it was someone arriving late for the feast, got up, took a sword in his hand, and opened the door. He could see no one outside, but thought that the person who had knocked might have gone back to join his company on the road, so he walked round the house to see. As he came past the woodpile, he heard the sound of horses' hoofs from the north, and saw nine women, dressed in black and with drawn swords in their hands, approaching on dark horses. Horses could also be heard approaching from the south, and from this direction came nine women in light clothes, on white horses.

Thidrandi was about to go back to call the others, when the women with dark horses bore down upon him and attacked him. He defended himself as well as he could, but when Thorhall discovered his absence and brought folk out to search for him, he was found lying on the ground, severely wounded. They carried him in, and he told them all that had happened, but before morning he was dead. Thorhall was asked for the cause of this terrible happening, and replied that he believed the women in black to be the guardian spirits of the family, who knew the fate which threatened them when Christianity came to Iceland. They were taking a final tribute from the family who would desert the old religion. The other white figures must have been the spirits of the new faith, who had not yet sufficient power to protect the victim.

There is an obvious resemblance here to the Christian tradition of angels and demons battling in the air for the soul of a dead man, as seen in a vision by St. Columba and others in the early Celtic church. The form which the vision takes, however, of two bands of women riding on horseback, is evidently based on the tradition of troops of valkyries or 'brides' of the heroes, of which we are told much in the literature.

Pagan martyrs

Sometimes those with power to see were said to behold a great and dazzling light burning around the Christian kings, or showing the place where a church was to stand. King Olaf Tryggvason was often represented as having magic powers, and was able to protect his followers on some enterprise, or bring down darkness and blindness on wizards who came to attack him, so that their evil spells recoiled on their own heads. It is under Olaf Tryggvason, in Norway, that we hear most concerning martyrs to the old faith. Particularly in Halogaland certain men refused to abandon the gods their families had long worshipped, and would not be baptised at the bidding of the king. Eyvind *kinnrifi* was said to have been tortured by the king with red-hot embers when he would not accept the Christian faith, declaring that he had been dedicated to the service of Odin and Thor by his parents, and he died rather than give way. Raud the powerful, another landowner in Halogaland, was also put to death by torture. He was said to be much skilled in magic, and it was from him that the king obtained the *Long Serpent*, his famous ship.

One of the most moving stories is that of Hallfred the Icelander, sent by King Olaf to blind the heathen seer, Thorleif the wise, whose wisdom and personality was such that the king could not find anyone who would carry out his bidding to kill or blind the man who refused to accept Christianity. Hallfred gained access to him in disguise, and succeeded in taking out one of his eyes, but he could not bring himself to rob him of the other, and told as much to the king, so that Thorleif was left, like Odin, with one eye only. Hakon Jarl, on the other

135

hand, did not choose to die a martyr. He consented to be baptised at the bidding of the Christian king Harald Greycloak, and was given a band of priests and learned men to take back with him to convert the north. But as soon as the wind was favourable, Hakon turned them all off his ship and sailed away before the king could stop him. He made a great sacrifice to Odin, saw two ravens flying overhead and screeching as they flew, and took this to be a sign that his sacrifice had been received by the god, and he could safely make war on the king. Hakon however was not dealing with the redoubtable Olaf, and at the time when he defied Harald, the heathen faith was still strong in Norway.

The missionary king

Olaf Tryggvason, who ruled Norway in the closing years of the tenth century, was a tough and ruthless opponent of heathenism and a powerful personality. He had been a fugitive from his enemies from birth, for his mother had to escape with him to Sweden to save his life, and later in boyhood he was captured by pirates and sold as a slave. He was found by a kinsman in a Russian slave-market, and grew to manhood in exile, afterwards going out on raiding expeditions to the British Isles. Some said that it was through a meeting with a Christian hermit in the Scilly Isles that he was converted, and when he got back the throne of Norway he proved an irresistible missionary for the new faith. He had great physical strength and courage, and was skilled in the accomplishments most admired by the Vikings. Under Olaf Tryggvason and his successor, Olaf the Holy, the Norwegians gradually gave up most of their heathen practices.

In Denmark a Christian priest, Poppo, succeeded in baptising Harald Gormsson in the tenth century, and the king set up a great stone on which was carved a vigorous and unusual representation of the crucifixion, the earliest known in Scandinavia. He converted the pagan sanctuary of his father, Gorm, with its two great burial mounds, into a place of Christian worship, and built a Christian church in the middle. Harald probably removed his parents from their grave in the northern mound into the new cathedral at Roskilde, for their burial chamber was found to be empty, while the other mound, no doubt intended for his own place of burial, was left with only a wooden framework to represent the house of the dead, instead of the wooden gravechamber in which he would have rested as a pagan king.

Conversion of Iceland

In Iceland it was said that after Thangbrand's stormy visit, and more serious missionary work by others, when Hall of the Side and a number of others had accepted Christianity, the new converts came to the Assembly and declared that they would no longer accept the heathen laws. The other men opposed them, but it was decided that the wisest of the lawmen, Thorgeir of Lightwater, should give the final decision, although he was a heathen. All day Thorgeir lay in silence, either meditating or in a trance, and next day he gave his answer. He declared that they must all share the same system of law, or there could be no peace in the land, and they all agreed to abide by his decision. Then he announced that it should be established by law that all accept the Christian faith, and be subject to outlawry if they worshipped the old gods publicly, although there should be no penalty for those who chose to keep up the heathen rites in private. In this way Christianity was accepted without bloodshed in the year A.D. 1000, the same year that Olaf Tryggvason went to his death on the *Long Serpent* in Norway. The men of Iceland accepted the fact that the new faith was now stronger than the old, and was the right path for them to follow.

Conversion of Northumbria

A similar decision, in a different setting, was described by the historian Bede some centuries earlier, when he wrote his account of the conversion of Northumbria in the year 625. King Edwin, the ruler of the recently united country and a great and successful king, was drawn towards the new faith, since he believed that it had been by the help of the Christian god that he had recovered his throne after many years of exile. His story and that of Olaf Tryggvason were rather similar. Both kings clearly felt that the luck and protection of the new god outweighed the powers of the old, since they had been pursued with all the hatred and determination of powerful heathen men, and had been delivered out of their hands.

Edwin moreover had a Christian wife, and had come under the influence of the priest she brought with her from Kent. When he put the problem to the council of wise men, the heathen priest himself put up no defence for the old gods, complaining that they had given him no fitting reward for long service. An unknown speaker is said to have put forward at this point a deeper and more moving plea for the new faith. All men, he said, lived a short time only on this earth, and went out into the darkness and uncertainty from which they came, like a bird going back into the cold and darkness of a winter's day after it has flown for a brief instant through the light and warmth of the king's hall. If any faith could give them greater hope and certainty in this perilous and unstable world, this was surely something which they must accept.

The strength of Christianity

The heathen faith was indeed in a weak position when it came up against the organised strength and deep convictions of the teachers of the Christian faith in the eleventh century in Scandinavia. The pagans had no central organisation, no fixed creed, and no firm beliefs for which men would be prepared to die. Those who opposed Christianity are shown to do so through a sense of loyalty to the past and to the faith of their fathers, and because they felt that Thor and Freyr had long helped and supported them. But few now retained any trust in Odin. The new faith could offer all that the old religion had given them: the ritual of the changing year, the help and counsel of Christ and his guardian angels, the support of mighty kings like Olaf the Holy, who became as it were a substitute for Thor, and was even shown with an axe in his hand, and the power of Christian mystics and seers to take the place of the wise men and women of heathen times. In addition Christianity brought with it a rich new symbolism and education by means of the written word, which meant so much to eager and ambitious youth. The discipline of the new faith, and the necessity to forwear all other beliefs when they accepted it, must have come as a shock to many, but it was too late now to turn back. Yet while in Scandinavia we find no great hostility towards the change of faith, there was still a great love of the old poems and stories, and the wealth of tradition about ancient kings and heroes and the achievements of the pagan past. It was due to this faithfulness to old memories of gods they had now forsworn that we find so many echoes of the world of myths in the art and literature of northern Europe.

Left: the interior of the stave church at Lom in Norway. In the oldest of these churches, the tops of the wooden pillars supporting the roof are the places for traditional carvings, some of them savage and impressive, and suggesting memories of pre-Christian symbolism.

Below left: figure on horseback set above one of the pillars in the stave church at Urnes. The rider appears to be a woman, and the spear she carries suggests memories of the fierce messengers of Odin who were sent down to carry out his commands on the battlefield.

Acknowledgments

The publishers gratefully acknowledge the following sources for permission to reproduce the illustrations indicated:

Colour Axel Poignant: 27 top, 98, 99, 103, 121. Bavaria Verlag: 34, 35. The Trustees of the British Museum, London: 54, 59, 73 top, 73 bottom. Gudmundur Hanneson: 124, 125. Michael Holford: 59 top. Holle Verlag: 34 left, 84 top. Institute of Archaeology, Oxford: 106, 125 top. National Museum, Copenhagen: 30, 31, 51, 77. National Historical Museum, Stockholm: Frontispiece, 55, 99 bottom, 125 bottom. Paul Hamlyn Archives: 27 bottom. Royal Norwegian Embassy: 129. Sheffield City Museum: 99 top. Universitetets Oldsaksamling, Oslo: 84 bottom, 102 and cover.

Black and White C. Andersen, Stockholm: 96 right. Antikvarisk - Topografiska Arkivet, Stockholm: 2, 3, 11, 16, 26 bottom, 27 bottom, 40 top and bottom, 41, 43, 44, 46, 47, 48, 49 left, 49 right, 65 left, 69, 72 bottom, 87, 92, 105, 107, 114 top, 128, 131 top, 132, 133. Author's Collection: 29. Axel Poignant: 61 right, 68, 93, 101, 104, 115, 120, 122, 123. Bavaria Verlag: 18, 19 top, 26, 62, 63, 86, 123 bottom, 127, 136 top and bottom. Trustees of the British Museum, London: 36, 60, 78 top, 91, 112. K. A. Carrdus, Oxford: 72 top. City of Liverpool Museums: 56 left. Danish Tourist Board, London: 18 bottom, 19 bottom, 89. Historisk Museum, Bergen: 14, 37. Kulturminnestadet, Goteburg: 39 bottom. The Manx Museum, 50, 108. National Museum, Copenhagen: 5, 17, 21, 24 right, 24 bottom, 30, 31, 32 top, 33 top, 38, 40 bottom, 58, 66, 67, 68, 69, 76, 78 bottom, 88, 90 right, 96 left, 97, 100. National Museum, Helsinki: 64 left, 134. National Museum of Iceland: 65 right, 130. National Historical Museum, Stockholm: 64 right, 128. National Travel Association of Denmark: 42. Count Oxenstierna, 61 left. Paul Hamlyn Archives: 79, 95 left and right. Ragnar Utne: 22 top and bottom, 23, 24, 25. Rijksmuseum van Oudheden, Leiden: 75. Riksantikvaren: 118, 119. Schleswig-Holsteinisches Landesmuseum: 53. Swedish Tourist Traffic Association, Stockholm: 90 left. Universitetets Oldsaksamling, Oslo: 13, 26 top, 32 bottom, 33 bottom, 39 top, 82, 83, 85, 109, 111, 113, 116, 117 left and right. University Museum of Archaeology and Ethnology, Cambridge: 70, 71. Uppsala University Museum: 15.

Further reading list

Almgren, O. *Nordische Felszeichnungen als religiöse Urkunden.* Verlag Moritz Diesterweg, Frankfurt, 1934.

Brøndsted, J. *Danmarks Oldtid* (2nd ed.), Gyldendalske Boghandel, Copenhagen, 1957-60.
The Vikings. Penguin Books, Harmondsworth, 1960.

Bruce-Mitford, R.L.S. *The Sutton Hoo Ship Burial.* Proc. Suffolk Inst. of Archaeology, XXV, 1949.

Davidson, H.R.E. *Gods and Myths of Northern Europe.* Penguin Books, Harmondsworth, 1964.
Pagan Scandinavia. Thames and Hudson, London, 1967.

Gelling, P. and Davidson, H.R.E. *The Chariot of the Sun.* Dent, London, 1969.

Grønbech, V. *The Culture of the Teutons.* Humphrey Milford, Oxford University Press, London, 1926.

Hawkes, S.C. *The Finglesham Man.* Antiquity XXXIX, 1965.

Jones, G. *A History of the Vikings.* Clarendon Press, Oxford, 1968.

Lid, N. *Scandinavian Heathen Cult Places.* Folk-Liv XXI-XXII, Stockholm, 1957-58.

Lindqvist, S. *Gotlands Bildsteine.* Kungl. Vitterhets Historie och Antikvitets Akademien, Stockholm, 1941-42.

Oxenstierna, Count E. *Die Goldhorner von Gallehus.* Lindingo, 1956.
The Norsemen, Studio Vista, London, 1966.
Poems of the Elder Edda. trans. L. Hollander. University of Texas Press, 1962.

Saxo Grammaticus. *Danish History.* Books 1-9 trans. by Lord Elton. Folklore Society, London, 1894.

Simpson, J. *Everyday Life in the Viking Age.* Batsford Books, London, 1966.

Snorri Sturluson. *The Prose Edda.* Selections trans. by Jean Young. Bowes and Bowes, Cambridge, 1954.

Stenburger, M. *Sweden*, Thames and Hudson, London, 1962.

Turville Petre, E.O.G. *Myths and Religion of the North.* Weidenfeld and Nicholson, London, 1964.

de Vries, J. *Altgermanische Religionsgeschichte* (2nd ed.), Walter de Gruyter, Berlin, 1956-67.

Index

Figures in italics refer to illustrations